ROLLING THE DICE IN DC

How the Federal Sales Game is Really Played

Richard White

Cover design: Thomas Luparello

Foreword

The federal government has an almost impossible job when it comes to buying products and services. The government makes over $390 billion worth of purchases annually, ranging from paper clips to space ships, and it often needs product and services overnight in response to natural disasters and acts of terrorism. Contracting organizations are under-funded, understaffed, and insufficiently trained and their contracting decisions are subject to scrutiny from Congress and the press. Yet it is Congress that writes the regulations and doesn't provide the funding.

The government has been forced out of necessity to implement value-based procurement rules and multi-vendor contract programs, both of which limit competition. The market was never completely competitive and it has gradually become less competitive over time.

The public tends to believe that the federal market is open to all because taxpayer money is being spent and they see public bid announcements. Political pressure, expediency, and the government's attitude of "let sleeping dogs lie" have contributed to the public's perception that the market is competitive. Many companies have tried to enter the market without success based on this general perception. While federal procurement officials do not intentionally mislead the public and the press about competitiveness, the truth is that the federal market is not all inclusive.

This book explains the federal sales game and how it is played in the real world. The market is insider dominated partly out of necessity and partly because procurement rules are outdated and Congress has not provided the funds to improve competitiveness.

The federal market is difficult to penetrate but, once you have cracked it, the market is extremely lucrative. Small businesses have a particularly hard time cracking the market. Yet small business preference programs can cause a start-up founded in someone's garage to grow to over $100 million dollars in revenue in a few short years. The chapters that follow will explain how a small business can make this happen.

This book is written for managers and sales people, not contract administrators. It describes the day-to-day dogfight of competing and winning in the federal market. Newcomers to the market may be discouraged by some of the topics and truths discussed. Continue reading if you want to know the good, bad, and the ugly of the federal market, what it takes to enter the market, and the potential returns. This book is not for you if you only want to know how to pick low-hanging federal fruit and whether there is a magic bullet for entering the federal market. The focus is selling, not how to comply with federal red tape and administer federal contracts. Win them and then worry about the red tap

The author is the CEO of Fedmarket.com and has more than forty years of experience in selling to the federal market. The following individuals collaborated on the content presented in this book:

- Matt Hankes, Vice President of Sales with Fedmarket.com

- Eileen Kent, Director of the Federal Sales Academy at Fedmarket.com

Some of the points in this book may appear a touch cynical but they are presented with tongue in cheek and in an effort to make a dry subject mildly interesting. The information presented is guaranteed to put you to sleep unless you are interested in making sales in the federal market.

For purposes of brevity, the federal government will sometimes be referred to as DC or the Beltway when, in fact, large federal purchases are made in your hometown and all over the world. Further, the book is about selling services and complex products or both. These types of sales will be referred to as selling a solution.

Table of Contents

Chapter 1

Growing Market

My editors tell me that federal procurement is a deadly, dull topic and I don't disagree. But it becomes more compelling if your paycheck depends on your knowledge of how the federal sales game is played or if your company is considering playing in the federal market.

Your Cheese Has Moved to DC

The amount of money the federal government spends on items such as the war in Iraq, disaster relief, and congressional pork-barrel projects is increasing at an unprecedented rate. Perhaps your company is considering going to D.C. to pick some of this low-hanging fruit. Unfortunately for the uninitiated, the fruit may be higher on the tree than you think and you may not have a complete understanding of the realities of selling in the federal market.

The World's Biggest Customer

The Washington Post recently reported that the country's defense and security spending is escalating more steeply than at any time in the past fifty years. The total size of these markets is difficult to pin down. Contract spending by federal agencies is compiled and made public two years after the fact and contract spending on intelligence programs remains hidden from public view. But economists and the Washington-based press estimate annual contract spending to be about $390 billion or more. The federal government is, in fact, the world's biggest customer.

Outsiders often have the misconception that the federal market exists only within the boundaries of the Capitol's Beltway. In fact, the Washington market includes the District of Columbia and the states of Maryland and Virginia. Although the actual Beltway is centered in the

Washington, DC area, the federal government's buying power extends across the United States and even worldwide because of overseas military bases and federal facilities.

Table 1 shows estimated contract spending amounts (inside and outside the Beltway) for Fiscal Year 2004 (ending September 30, 2005). The spending amounts should be viewed as approximations. The numbers were culled from the Federal Procurement Data System, which is notorious for underreporting contract spending data.

Table 1 - Contract Spending Inside and Outside the Beltway (Dollars in Billions)

Geographic Area	Department of Defense	Department of Energy	Other Agencies	Totals
Inside Beltway (DC, MD, & VA)	$ 36.1	$ 0.7	$ 29.6	$ 66.4
Outside Beltway (All States Except DC, MD, & VA)	169.9	19.3	31.4	220.6
All States	206	20	61	287
Outside U.S.	18	2	--	20
Total All States & Outside U.S.	224	22	61	307
Individual States				
California	27.8	2.4	8.1	38.3
Tennessee	2.1	3.0	1.0	6.1
New Mexico	1.0	4.4	0.5	5.9

The enormity of the federal spending numbers reflects the trend to outsource traditionally governmental functions to commercial companies. Over the last several decades, the federal government has outsourced almost everything, including the maintenance of military bases, space shuttle operations, the operation and management of Department of Energy (DOE) research laboratories, security guard services, and public relations services.

Most newcomers to the federal market do not realize that an average of $221 billion dollars is spent annually outside of the Beltway. This money may be spent at a military base or other government installations in your state. Most states receive the majority of their federal contracting dollars from the Department of Defense (DOD). DOE also contributes greatly to the coffers of a number of states. In fact, the states receiving the bulk of DOE dollars are those that are the home to DOE research laboratori (such as the Oak Ridge National Laboratory in Tennessee and the Los Alamos and Sandia National Laboratories in New Mexico). California ha received the largest benefit from federal government spending, and has the luxury of hosting several military bases and three DOE laboratories.

A June 2006 report by the United States House of Representatives, Committee on Government Reform, Minority Staff, Special Investigatior Division entitled "Dollars, Not Sense: Government Contracting under th Bush Administration," summarizes the growth in the federal market. Although a trifle political, the following excerpt paints a realistic picture (federal spending:

"President Bush came into office promising to reduce the size of the federal government, but he has presided over a large expansion of the federal role. Under his Administration, the fastest-growing component o government is the 'shadow government' represented by private compani doing public work under federal contract. In 2000, the federal government spent $203.1 billion on contracts with private companies. By 2005, this spending had soared to $377.5 billion. During this period, spending on federal contracts grew at nearly double the rate of other discretionary federal spending. Almost half of the growth in discretionary spending between 2000 and 2005 can be attributed to increased expenditures on private contractors.

This procurement spending is concentrated on the largest private contractors. The top five recipients of federal contracts -- Lockheed Martin, Boeing, Northrop Grumman, Raytheon, and General Dynamics received $80 billion in 2005, more than 21% of the total federal contract dollars. Just twenty corporations received 36% of the total dollars awarded in 2005. Lockheed Martin, the largest federal contractor, receive $25 billion in 2005, more than the budgets of the Department of Commerce, the Department of Interior, the Small Business Administration, and Congress combined."

Should We or Shouldn't We

Should you join the parade to grab some of these contracting opportunities? The federal government has always been an extremely lucrative market; world events are just making it more visible. As with everything in life, you can't just pick up federal contract dollars and put them in a bag. Those of you with battle scars from the sales game probably realize that tackling the federal market will require a substantial investment of money and time. Some have tried to take short cuts and are now waking up every morning in a prison cell (or at home anxiously awaiting appellate court rulings).

You should probably stay where you are if you are in the oil business or are a Wall Street suit. Otherwise, consider selling to the federal government. Those who decide to go forward must commit significant resources to their sales program and also be prepared to wait at least one year for their first dollar of federal revenue. All it takes is money and the knowledge gleaned from this book, of course.

Most federal sales, like commercial sales, start with a customer relationship. To be successful in the market, you must consider the entire sales cycle as a business process. Many outsiders think that they can jump into the middle of the process. Because the federal government publicizes its bidding opportunities at a central web site, companies hoping to win business with the government think they can simply conduct a search and pick and choose projects to bid on.

As you may have surmised, jumping in the middle doesn't work. In order to be successful in the federal market, your sales staff must (i) make direct sales calls to establish trust relationships with end users, and (ii) learn to play the "close the sale" game. The game is really not that different than the game played in the commercial market. The difference with the federal market is that there's much more paper work.

As in the commercial sector, insiders dominate the federal market. Ensconced insiders devoted significant company time and money to establish the necessary business relationships with federal buyers. Those new to the market need to understand the long-term investment required to become an insider.

You will need to invest in a direct sales program, be patient, and stay focused on the goal. Once you win that first federal contract, you will have become an insider and have all the advantages that come with reaching that status. Federal government customers will send you repeat business if you perform well and the resulting impact on corporate revenue can be dramatic. Businesses have been built from scratch and have grown to annual revenue in the hundreds of millions of dollars by doing just that.

The federal market presents unlimited opportunities as long as your management has a complete understanding of the market. The federal buyer's aversion to risk and the resulting loyalty to good performers can result in dramatic increases in your corporate revenue. Although it is the most difficult market to tackle, the potential benefits greatly outweigh the risks involved in doing business in the federal market.

Play by the Rules

There is no getting around it. The federal government is a monstrous bureaucracy. The federal rules concerning competition for contracts and how the federal government buys have changed significantly over the past ten years. The new rules seek to eliminate (or minimize to the largest extent possible) red tape to make federal buying faster and more efficient. Under recent rule changes, the government has defined a new category of "commercial" products that can be purchased quickly and with less paperwork. The revised rules also expanded the government's multiple-vendor contract programs. This type of contract allows an agency's buyer to place orders with companies that are pre-qualified to handle government business at pre-approved prices.

As with the older versions of the procurement rules, the new rules favor both the government and insiders. Generally, the government plays the purchasing game as you would if you were in their shoes. Government buyers go with the proven, trusted source.

On the other hand, the government does have the best interest of the taxpayer at heart. With recent natural disasters in mind, most citizens would prefer that the government possess the ability to buy necessary products and services quickly. The multiple-award contract system attempts to address these concerns. No one has figured out a better way to buy under the conflicting constraints of our system. So let's accept the rules and play by them.

Who Would Have Guessed?

Federal funding of new ventures parallels the rush by the private sector to solve government problems. In-Q-Tel was created in 1999 as a private, independent organization tasked with assisting the CIA and the Intelligence Community in developing and acquiring cutting-edge technologies. This fund has invested in more than a hundred companies since its inception. The Army formed OnPoint Technologies in 2003. In 2005, the National Aeronautics and Space Administration established the Mercury Fund. Currently, the Navy is considering its own fund and more agencies are expected to jump on the venture capital bandwagon.

Who would have guessed that the staid old federal government would jump into the venture capital business? It is truly becoming a Silicon Beltway.

Playing the federal sales game can be frustrating and rewarding. Don't roll the dice in DC unless you know how the game is really played. Otherwise you will be taking unnecessary risks with your hard-earned dollars.

Chapter 2

The Market: Truths and Misconceptions

The federal market can be an alien and confusing world. Many would-be contractors firmly believe that federal bureaucracies are governed by strange and convoluted procurement rules designed to confuse and even intimidate. The market appears big and mysterious from the outside and this creates misconceptions about how federal business is done. The mystery dissolves once you are on the inside and have learned how to pla the game.

Companies entering the federal market find that it is essentially the same as the commercial market. You have to find out who buys what you sell, knock on their door, be prepared for rejection if you are unknown to the federal buyers, and then find a way to get around their resistance to newcomers. In the federal market, as in the commercial market, businesses must sell to the end users of the product or service they offer. The difference with the federal market is that it is critical that you have a way to <u>close</u> the sale.

The competitiveness of the federal market is a frequent topic of conversation inside the Beltway because the amount of competition and the rules governing purchasing decisions are critical to how a sale is made Full and open competition is rare in the federal market. The lack of full and open competition is not an indictment of the federal acquisition system, because in most cases it is not really in the best interests of the taxpayer.

Full and open competition is not cost-effective and inherently lengthens the time required to make a purchase. The goal of the federal acquisition system is to maximize competition consistent with providing best value for taxpayers. That having been said, federal contracting officials and industry representatives are also aware of the need to make the market more open and receptive to outsiders.

People Buy, Not Agencies

Contrary to popular belief, people buy in the federal market, not agencies. The only way to make a federal sale is to contact a buyer through a direct sales call. Companies unwilling to make the sales calls are not going to experience success in the market.

Although rules and regulations often tie a government buyer's hands, they don't turn the buyer into a robot. Government buyers are people with the same general motivations and inclinations we all have, rules or no rules. Government end users buy from vendors they know and trust. The government employee's success and future promotions depend on the value of the products and services they buy and, because of that, they want to be assured that their vendors will perform well.

It's not just about getting the best deal for the taxpayer. Although certainly a factor, "taxpayer protection" is often a fuzzy, nebulous concept. The reality is that the federal buyer wants to get the deal that works best for him and his superiors. From a federal buyer's perspective, a good deal is one in which risk is minimized.

Federal end users, such as human resource program managers, engineers, or facility managers, make most purchasing decisions. As the term implies, the end user is the person who will actually use the service. Services and complex products and solutions must be sold to the end user because this person is the one who determines if the service or product meets their needs and solves their problem.

An official buyer, also known as a contracting officer, is positioned within the agency's contracting division. Contracting officers are charged with the legal responsibility for making purchases and ensuring that the purchases are made within the boundaries of the procurement rules. Contracting officers work with end users to transact a purchase, but it is the contracting officer who signs the contract with the vendor.

It is the contracting officer's duty to make sure that the buying process is as competitive as possible. However, the contracting officer also has the latitude to take into consideration the factors surrounding the procurement. "Factors" is the operative word here. Factors that can affect the contracting officer's final decision include the dollar amount of the buy, when the product or service is needed, the type of businesses competing, the qualifications of the bidders and more.

In instances in which commodities are being purchased (such as office supplies), contracting officers are often the sole decision makers. In selling commodities, contracting officers should be viewed as end users.

Many companies entering the federal market believe that federal agencies will automatically place orders with vendors who hold pre-approved price lists such as a GSA Schedule contract. With the possible exception of the purchase of mass-produced products, this is untrue. The government doesn't place orders with vendors listed in some magical central database. Products and services are sold by people to people. You must sell an end user first and then close the sale within the government's purchasing rules.

Closing a Sale

Making sales in the commercial sector can be difficult but closing a sale usually isn't. In the commercial sector, a senior manager works with vendors to decide what product best suits his or her company's needs and then makes the purchase using a credit card or, in the case of a high-dollar transaction, the purchase is consummated by the company's purchasing department. Actually making the purchase once a decision has been made is relatively simple.

Making a purchase in the federal arena is not that simple. The process is the same up to the point of completing the transaction. The end user in the federal arena may meet with one or more vendors and obtain information about the features, benefits, and past performance of a company's product or service. The end user then meets with the contracting officer, who will ask how much money is involved and will remind the end user of the necessity for strict adherence to applicable procurement rules. This is where the process becomes complex.

The following summarizes the methods in which a federal purchase can be closed or transacted:

- A credit card buy (the quickest and simplest)

- The issuance of a purchase order for amounts under $25,000; the federal purchaser must first obtain three quotes (relatively simple)

- A public bid (long, lengthy, expensive, and to be avoided if possible)

- A multi-vendor contract that allows the government to purchase from a select list of vendors who are pre-qualified (including pre-negotiated prices) in anticipation of future purchasing needs

- A subcontract with a prime contractor that already has a federal contract

- A subcontract with a "preferred" small business that the government can contract with quickly and with limited competition (e.g., a small disadvantaged business, Alaskan Native Corporation, etc.)

The manner in which a purchase is completed depends on the size of the transaction. Credit card buys under $2,500 can be single sourced by the end user and can be transacted without the contracting officer's involvement. More liberal credit card limits apply in emergency and national security situations.

For purchases in the $2,500 to $25,000 range, the federal purchaser must obtain quotes from three vendors to meet the "best value determination" required under procurement rules.

Purchases exceeding $25,000 are made either through a public bid process or through a multiple vendor contract. Public bids are open to everyone and the process is lengthy--the average time from posting a bid to contract award is more than two hundred days. From the government's perspective, a public bid is an expensive process requiring considerable, and often unavailable, staff resources. If nothing else, Hurricane Katrina demonstrated how inefficient the government's public bid process can be. Vital services that were needed in response to the emergency could not be procured quickly and efficiently.

Why would the government select a public bid as the closing procedure of choice given the horrendous lead time and cost? Contracting officers do their very best to avoid them. Although it is true that public bids are the method of last resort, a project is often so large and publicly visible that a public procurement is the only acceptable procedure as far as vendors, the taxpayer and the press are concerned. In rare instances, a public bid is issued when a vendor has sold an opportunity but doesn't have an appropriate closing procedure. Unfortunately, putting a contract out for bid may be the only option when a desired vendor doesn't have a closing mechanism.

Purchases in excess of $25,000 can also be made through companies holding multi-vendor contracts (such as GSA Schedule contracts). Multi-vendor contracts allow the government to purchase from pre-qualified vendors using pre-negotiated prices. Bids are usually solicited from three or more vendors holding such a contract and the successful vendor is selected from that list. Purchases made through multi-vendor contracts are quick and cost effective for the government. From the vendor's perspective, competition is minimized and a deal can be closed quickly.

Companies holding multi-vendor contracts minimize the amount of competition they face since a public bid isn't necessary. Vendors who don't hold a multi-vendor contract may have to start out as a subcontractor to an existing federal contractor, commonly called a "prime contractor," in order to close a sale. For example, your company could sell a product or service to an end user at a particular agency and the agency may decide that the best way to close your sale is through a subcontract with a trusted prime contractor (as opposed to going through a lengthy and expensive public bid process). The prime contractor may already have a contract with the agency or hold a multi-vendor contact that can be used to close the sale.

Subcontracting is a valid way to close a sale but it has drawbacks. The primary drawback is that a subcontract with a prime contractor doesn't give you your first step toward achieving insider status. When acting as a subcontractor, you do not have a contract with the federal government. Instead your business has a commercial contract with the prime contractor. The prime contractor controls your company's prices, your sales growth, and your destiny with the federal customer. A savvy prime contractor also insulates the federal customer from its subcontractors so the subcontractors never really achieve insider status.

GSA Schedule contracts are the best closing mechanisms for small and medium-sized businesses that cannot afford to hold several multi-vendor contracts. Under a GSA Schedule contract, the federal government and the vendor agree to pre-approved prices for the vendor's products and services. More importantly, such contracts are quick and easy for any federal agency to use.

Keep in mind that GSA Schedule vendors still need to sell the end user just as they would in the commercial sector. Newcomers should start the process of obtaining a GSA Schedule contract immediately upon deciding to enter the market because it can take three to nine months, or more, to get an award of such a contract.

A variation on the prime contractor/subcontractor approach to closing a sale is to become a subcontractor to a small business under one of the federal government's many small business preference programs. These programs allow quick purchases with preferred types of small businesses under rules allowing limited competition.

A sole-source contract is another alternative for closing a sale; however sole sourcing is extremely rare unless there is truly only a single source for a product or service. Among other challenges, sole-source contracts require special, hard-to-obtain approval from above. The government does its best to keep such contracts under the public's radar.

Is the Federal Playing Field Level?

The answer to this question is yes, in theory, but no in practice. The federal market is open to a degree but in a much different way than most people outside the market understand.

The Federal Acquisition Regulation (FAR) contains the rules that federal procurement personnel must follow when buying products and services. The rules have been gradually loosened and made more realistic in the past ten years. Contracting officers have more latitude than under earlier rules. While federal agencies publicly embrace full and open competition, the government would grind to a halt if that were the reality.

Federal buyers are charged with the task of getting the best value for the taxpayer. Depending on the situation, getting the best value does not always mean encouraging competition. The commercial sector would not operate efficiently if it bought everything using full and open competitive purchasing procedures and the federal government is no different.

Buying services and solutions is inherently less competitive than buying a product because of the many risk factors involved and the need for the customer to understand what they are buying. The federal government has always experienced problems with the lack of competition in buying services and solutions. It is the same in the commercial sector because buyers are purchasing an intangible at considerable risk. Would you take the lowest bid for heart surgery?

Products that have defined features and benefits, like toner cartridges, laser printers, and computer monitors, lend themselves to competitive procurements. Products based on complex technologies with many optional features and capabilities -- commercial off-the-shelf software, scientific computers, network routers -- tend to be less competitive.

The level of competition in the federal sector depends on the number of vendors pre-selling the opportunity. Ten large system integrators might go head-to-head for a billion-dollar procurement, while there may be only one real bidder for a smaller database maintenance buy. It also depends heavily on whether there is an incumbent contractor or the buy is a new opportunity. Operations and management contracts of any type -- maintaining an army base, building a space shuttle, feeding the soldiers in Iraq -- are probably the least competitive because there is almost always an incumbent contractor.

Federal purchases of commodity products (such as those for copier paper, tools, printer cartridges, paper shredders) tend to be less competitive than similar purchases in the commercial sector. End users and contracting officers focus more on obtaining bids from several vendors than on getting the lowest price. The federal market is not profit driven and federal rules do not always benefit the lowest bidder.

Contract bundling reduces competitiveness dramatically. What does a contracting organization do when it is understaffed? It bundles and gets everything done in one fell swoop. Procurements addressing new issues and existing contracts can be combined into one large procurement opportunity and contracted through a public bid or a multi-vendor contract. The larger and more varied the scope of work, the more likely it is to be awarded to a large, established prime contractor. The rich get richer.

Are Federal Bids Wired?

A common perception about federal public bids is that they are "wired," implying that the bid is set up or rigged to favor a particular company. They are not wired in that sense but in a practical sense they may favor the incumbent contractor or one or more companies that have done the following:

- Convinced the end user, through pre-selling, that they offer a superior product or service

- Taken the time to get to know the agency and the specific requirements of the procurement through pre-selling or through having done prior work for the agency

- Demonstrated in previous contracts with an agency that they are proven performers

- Proven to the agency, through references from other customers, that they are a reputable vendor

Most public competitions involve many companies although the number of companies with a real chance of winning will be few. The true contenders will usually have one or more of the characteristics listed above. Keep this in mind when your business is considering bidding on a public procurement. The question each business should ask is whether it has been aggressively pre-selling the opportunity and has personally met with the customer. If the answer to this question is "no," then don't waste your time and money bidding on a contract that is open to the public. It isn't.

Purchases made through public bids represent a relatively small percentage of buys made in the federal market. More often, purchases are made through multiple award schedule contracts or modifications to existing federal contracts.

An opportunity may be put out for public bid if:

- The agency knows a number of companies have been aggressively pre-selling the opportunity and the only option, from a political standpoint, is to conduct a public bid

- The project is large and highly visible

- The vendor the agency wants to work with doesn't have a GSA Schedule contract and there isn't a prime contractor available to use as a conduit

- The contract that was originally bid publicly comes up for re-bid

- The agency needs to pad its public bid numbers

- The agency truly doesn't have a vendor pre-selected (yes, this happens on occasions)

Don't bid on a public procurement if you haven't done significant advance research. A bidder must have all of the background information in order to understand the nuances of the deal. There is always a back story and the vendor which eventually wins the contract will have uncovered all of the intelligence well in advance of the posting of the bid

The Glass Wall

Companies new to the federal market usually run into a glass wall because they haven't had sufficient time to develop relationships with the end users. Federal customers, like their counterparts in the commercial sector, want to know the companies and the people with whom they will be working. Building these personal relationships requires making direct sales calls. Direct sales are, to say the least, difficult when you do not hav network contacts and established relationships. This is the single biggest deterrent to businesses entering the market.

The Thick Wall

Establishing relationships with federal customers can be a long, arduous process that can often take a year or more. The federal end user's job depends on the vendors he chooses and, as a result, the end user is often averse to taking a risk with an unproven vendor.

Unfortunately, there's no magic bullet or shortcut that makes the endeavor easier. Use any federal relationship that you have and, if none exist, make repeated cold calls until you get in the door. Consider leveraging relationships you have with federal prime contractors to sell your services to them as a subcontractor. If you don't have such relationships, make the same cold calls until you have established contact

You have to be willing to make the investment to get through the glass wall. The federal sales cycle is long, but persistence and focused, direct sales efforts pay off in the long run. You become an insider when you win your first contract. Once you have achieved that status, it can be used to leverage sales growth.

Can Others Help?

It helps if you can find someone to pave the way. The best candidate would be someone, such as a business partner or personal friend, who has a federal customer. Government small business specialists or congresspersons are usually not the best candidates to assist you.

The government gives the impression that it will pave the way for small businesses. Although federal buyers need to contract with small businesses, they are reluctant to do so if they don't have past experience with those vendors. Your congressional representative might help if there are votes or campaign contributions involved or if a project benefits your district or his or her constituents.

Although it certainly can't hurt to ask agencies like the Small Business Administration, contracting officers, or even your state senator or congressperson for help, you need to have a realistic view of what assistance might be forthcoming. Furthermore, you cannot rely on them to make sales calls for you. Counting on the government for help can divert you from making critical, direct sales calls. Don't get sidetracked by thinking that others will sell for you.

The Bright Side

Once you get through the glass wall, you can sell based on value rather than on price. And best value is defined broadly in the FAR. My father used to say, "Son, you get what you pay for." In the past, federal government buyers made purchasing decisions based primarily on price considerations. While price is still important, the government has modernized its regulations to allow buying decisions based on best value.

As a taxpayer, you should be happy about best value purchasing decisions. As a sales person, it's an answer to your prayers. It gives government buyers the latitude to use their judgment and the sales person the opportunity to sell quality, features, benefits, results, and past performance. All of these factors can be considered in determining best value. Direct sales will pay off in the long run as long as you are selling quality and value.

Become an Incumbent Contractor and Get Paid to Sell

Once you make a sale, you can use your company's stellar performance on a federal project to leverage more sales. Federal contractors working on-site at a federal facility are essentially getting paid to sell to agency customers and to generate profit at the same time. Their billable staff sits with the customer every day and, in most cases, gains invaluable intelligence about that customer. Their on-site staff has the opportunity to learn everything there is to know about the customer, the customer's problems, possible fixes, the agency's budget, the agency's procurement plans and the like. It's all perfectly legal because it is all public information. In this instance, the insider just has much easier access to it.

More importantly, a contractor's on-site personnel establish friendships and strong relationships with federal customers by just doing their job. We have repeatedly stressed that establishing such relationships is critical to success in the federal market and the on-site contractor gets paid to do it. If you were the customer, to whom would you turn if you needed help You would turn to the people with whom you are working every day, people you know and trust.

The federal government doesn't really have a practical way of eliminating the inherent insider edge. It could prohibit the incumbent contractor from re-bidding on their existing contracts but this would be disruptive, expensive, and not in the taxpayers' best interests. Paradoxically, information technology and consulting companies paid to write the specifications for a federal bid are prohibited from bidding on the procurement, even though they are likely to have the most in-depth understanding of both the problem and the solution.

In summary, your company will eventually land federal customers if your business has focus, your sales people have a total lack of fear and are impervious to rejection, and your corporate management shows patience. A federal customer is like a piece of gold. Because end users and contracting officers are risk averse, they will come back to you again and again if you perform well. People buy in the federal market just like in the commercial market. Find an end user with a problem and establish a trust relationship with them.

Chapter 3

The Book of Rules

From a sales perspective, procurement rules concerning the sale of products and services to federal buyers can be easily and succinctly summarized in one sentence. It is as follows:

Vendors are encouraged to meet with federal end users before a purchase is publicly announced.

The book of rules governing federal purchases is called the Federal Acquisition Regulation (FAR) which can be found at http://www.acqnet.gov/far/. The FAR is as thick as the Bible and reads like the convoluted, bewildering document you would expect to see when lawyers and politics mix. One quote from the FAR says it all:

"All participants in the (Federal Acquisition) System are responsible for making acquisition decisions that deliver the best value product or service to the customer. Best value must be viewed from a broad perspective and is achieved by balancing the many competing interests in the System. The result is a system which works better and costs less."

Clear as mud, right? The goal is to get the best deal for the taxpayer. To do this, end users must know the features and benefits of what they are buying in order to make intelligent, effective purchasing decisions. The public must be confident that services and products are being bought wisely and fairly. At a practical level, promoting competition is not necessarily consistent with achieving best value.

The FAR has only a few parts that truly affect how you sell in the federal market. The most important rules in the FAR from a sales perspective are the rules governing seller and buyer communications and best value vendor selection.

Buyer-Seller Communications

Sales of products and services have been based on buyer-seller relationships since the cave man. Anyone purchasing a complex product or service knows that you don't buy unless you know what you are buying and the product's value to you. Even if you were buying something as simple as paper clips, you would need to know that they meet industry standards, that they will be delivered in a timely fashion, and that you were getting a reasonable discount for a bulk purchase.

This information cannot be communicated solely through the written word. Personal communication between the buyer and seller is essential and this is true both in the commercial and governmental sectors.

Those outside of the federal market generally believe that the government buys through full and open competition. It may be open but, at a practical level, it can't be full. Federal agencies don't have the personnel, time, or resources to conduct in-depth reviews of hundreds of proposals submitted by companies they've never heard of. End users are much more comfortable with looking at the five to ten bids from companies with a track record with the end user. Thus, the competition takes place when relationships are built--during the sales call -- not when a public bid is advertised and proposals are requested.

How does the federal government attempt to satisfy the conflicting objectives of making a fully-informed purchasing decision while still keeping the process fair? Can a vendor take an end user out to lunch? Invite him over for dinner? Send him on an all-expenses paid trip to Hawaii?

Use your common sense. Know that there is a line, and don't step over it. And I'm not talking about buying lunches here. Almost everyone knows that you don't buy lunches or provide any favors of value. Meeting with federal end users about their requirements, problems, and possible solutions is encouraged, but all communication must end once procurement is formally announced. Your company should be in good shape if you have done your homework and established a strong relationship before the Request for Proposal is published.

Excerpts from the FAR discuss the rules about meeting with vendors before receipt of proposals:

- Exchanges of information among all interested parties, from the earliest identification of a requirement through receipt of proposals, are encouraged.

- Techniques to promote early exchanges of information include one-on-one meetings with potential offerors. (Meetings dealing with potential contract terms and conditions should include the contracting officer.) Editor's note - The term "offeror" means you.

- After release of the solicitation, the contracting officer must be the focal point of any exchange with potential offerors.

To summarize the excerpts provided above, pre-selling before a bid is announced publicly is not only allowed, it is encouraged. The federal procurement system can't work without meetings between vendors and end users.

My reading of the FAR can be summed up as follows: We want you to meet with end users while the need for a product or service is being identified and formulated. We'd even be happy to meet you before we know we have a need for a particular service or product. But we are closing the barn door immediately upon publication of the buy.

It really can't be done any other way. Full and open competition just takes far too long and has to be limited as a practical matter. The rules are written to reflect this reality.

Best Value Selection

The FAR gives federal buyers flexibility and considerable latitude in making a purchasing decision. Under the FAR, the term "best value" means the expected outcome of an acquisition provides the greatest overall benefit in response to the requirement. In short, the rules give contracting officers the latitude to:

1. Go with a higher price based on best value considerations, with no restrictions on what best value considerations have to be. Anything can be considered a best value factor as long as it makes sense and has cost and performance implications.

2. Consider time and the cost of the procurement itself when determining how to make a buy.

The government holds all of the cards and can do just about anything it wants in making a buy as long as it appears to be cost effective and in the best interests of the taxpayer. Most buyers make rational decisions, are not out to harm vendors, and do not like to be viewed as unfair. The downside to federal contracting is that if you feel you have been wronged there is very little you can do about it. You can protest using a formal process if you think procurement rules have been violated but the chance of winning a protest are slim to none.

Chapter 4

The People in the Process and How They Are Motivated

Buyers in the commercial and federal sectors behave in the same manner. Most buyers will choose the path of least resistance and then run to get to their kids' soccer games on time. Federal buyers view obtaining the best value for the taxpayer as a noble objective but hold doing the best to maximize their raises and performance evaluations on an even higher plane.

Experienced sales people selling in the federal market know that the roles people play and their motivations profoundly affect buying decisions. Most people are motivated by self-interest; that's not necessarily a good or bad thing, it's just a fact. The desire to do a good job, to avoid failure, and to save money on behalf of the taxpayer benefits us all. Having a clear picture of the various roles of the people in the federal sales game may help you better target your sales approach.

Person	Responsibilities	Primary Motivation	Not Motivated To:
Federal end user	Performing a job for the taxpayer in the most efficient, cost-effective manner possible	Successfully accomplishing work tasks and being rewarded with raises and promotions	Select an unknown vendor or one who represents a potential risk
	Monitoring contractor performance	Avoiding risk, ensuring that buying decisions produce the desired outcome	
Contracting officer	Legal responsibility for a contract (signs contract)	Successfully accomplishing work tasks and being	Contract with a vendor which was selected in violation

Person	Responsibilities	Primary Motivation	Not Motivated To:
	Ensuring that requirements for competitive bids have been met Monitoring contract performance	rewarded with raises and promotions Ensuring that all rules and regulations have been followed Maintaining a contract file that shows maximum possible competition took place	of the rules
Small business specialist (advocate)	Advocating the use of small businesses	Promoting the use of small businesses as a policy	Help a particular small business win contract
Members of Congress and the White House	Develop and pass legislation Represent constituents Contract performance	Re-election Votes and campaign dollars Bring major projects into their own states or districts More contract dollars Controlling the customer relationship	Help a particular small business win contract unless the exercise is directly connected to more votes or money Subcontract with companies that do not bring contract dollars or that threaten the customer relationship

Who Sells

The level of corporate participation on a particular transaction depends on the type of product or service being sold, the size of the company, and the dollar value of the procurement. Deals involving millions or billions of dollars frequently involve the CEO of a company, along with a supporting cast of many full- and part-time salespeople. The sales investment in large projects can be in the millions.

Vice presidents or partners usually take the lead in selling large, professional service projects because the end user wants to know the person or persons who will be responsible for contract performance. Many companies employ sales and marketing people, commonly called business development specialists, to identify opportunities and schedule meetings. Low-cost commodities can be sold over the phone by members of your sales staff.

How the sales function is performed varies by what is being sold. Although the frequency and manner of customer contact can range from one or two telephone calls to many face-to-face meetings, the goal is always the same. Your focus should be on raising the end user's awareness of, and comfort level with, your company and the product or service you are selling.

How Purchasing Decisions Are Made

Like all of us, the people who make buying decisions in the federal government are influenced by their own biases, perceptions, and views of the world. Although the government uses an ostensibly objective numeric scoring system to evaluate proposals, in the end it's a person who assigns the score. It's not much different from when your teachers graded you way back when. A proposal evaluator reads a submitted resume and decides the person on the resume is graded out at a score of 87 out of 100. Why not an 85 or 89? Because it is a subjective process and all procurement decisions boil down to a subjective judgment no matter how sophisticated the scoring scheme.

Scoring usually doesn't occur when products are purchased, but essentially the same thing happens. A buyer may say that product pricing, a particular feature, fast delivery time, or the availability of an extended warranty is his basis for selecting Product A over Product B. In fact, Product A and B may be virtually identical; the difference is that the seller of Product A employed a more effective sales approach. Whether buying one million paperclips or a $10 million software system, the most important factor in making the sale is usually what the buyer has learned from salespeople. A salesperson's goal is to make a sale by helping buyers make informed decisions.

Information garnered from a vendor's references, from colleagues who have past experience with a vendor, and the general reputation and brand identity of the vendor all contribute to what comes down to a buyer's subjective decision based on value.

Trench Warfare

People on the outside do not realize what goes on when contracts worth millions to billions of dollars are at stake. Sales efforts can be likened to trench warfare and the meek inherit very little. When a large federal contract is known to be in the pre-announcement phase, interested prime contractors send teams of people to the federal agency. Prime contractor will establish sales budgets ranging from $100,000 to several million dollars when large opportunities -- such as DOE research laboratory management projects or lucrative information technology service opportunities -- are announced.

The "capture planning teams" descend on the federal site and spend countless hours meeting with each other to form the optimum bidding team. Points of discussion include exclusivity, how team members will share the work, oversight and accountability issues, the dollars involved, and the guarantees (if any) associated with a vendor's share of the pot. Prime contractors and potential subcontractors are usually jockeying to get the best deal and may not be telling each other the full story.

Prime contractors may woo small businesses thought to be in favor with the agency putting out the bid. The teams also meet with the end users to gather intelligence on the problems, requirements, fears, likes, and dislike and to sell themselves to the government decision makers. Remember, this is legal prior to formal announcement of the procurement.

Phone calls are made to anyone and everyone who might know about the project in an effort to discern the makeup of the evaluation committee, the favored parties, which players may be on what team and why. Companies search for any insight that might provide an edge. Great effort is put into recruiting the incumbent contractor's personnel since the government usually wants all or most of the key people to remain on the contract.

All of this work is focused on structuring a scheme to win the contract. This is not a game for the faint hearted or inexperienced company. Once the procurement is formally announced and the proposal is written, prayer, pacing, and worrying are the order of the day.

Sounds like white-collar warfare, doesn't it? This is where the competition actually takes place. To outsiders it may sound illegal or unethical but it isn't as long as all the game playing is done before the government issues the bid solicitation.

Who wins? Usually the incumbent contractor provided there is one. If the project is new, the winner is the vendor with the strongest relationship with the end users, or the one which has been the most aggressive, persuasive, creative, or a mixture of all of these factors. A vendor without a relationship can sneak in and build a winning proposal right under the nose of the lead contender by being aggressive and creative. However, to do so requires a formidable commitment of time, resources, and money (not to mention a healthy share of luck).

Press Posturing

A relatively new form of competition, press posturing, has recently emerged. The first two paragraphs of an article from *Washington Technology* magazine titled "Raytheon vows immediate results on SBI-Net" illustrates how the game is played.

> "Raytheon Co. officials today pledged to move quickly, offer the best value and use only proven technologies if they win the contract for the $2 billion Secure Border Initiative-Network border surveillance system from the Homeland Security Department.

> The Raytheon-led team expects to leverage its experience as a prime integrator on a similarly huge remote surveillance network in Brazil and rely on existing technologies and telecommunications infrastructure available from its major partners in the project, including Bechtel Co., Verizon Inc. and Alltel Corp." (7/19/2006)

This article demonstrates the many avenues a company might use to influence a purchasing decision. I expect that unless the newspapers balk, we will soon be bombarded with contractor-issued press releases touting the company's wares and capabilities. Or advertising will be mixed with news so it is difficult to tell the difference. Incidentally, the Boeing Company was awarded the SBI-Net contract in September 2006.

Chapter 5

Multiple Vendor Contracts

If you already know all there is to know about multi-vendor contracts and their intrinsic value, consider skipping this chapter. Read on if, like most, the word makes you cringe and you have little or no knowledge about the subject.

The federal government has put an increasing emphasis on a type of pre-negotiated contract that is awarded to a number of vendors before specific purchasing requirements are known (called a "multi-vendor contract"). When the need for a product or service arises, the end user can turn to the list of pre-approved vendors and make a purchase quickly and efficiently. The time and expense involved with a public bid are avoided because the vendors holding this type of contract have agreed-upon price lists which become the basis for bids on individual task orders (services) or delivery orders (products).

Multi-vendor contracts are gradually becoming the federal government's preferred method for buying products and services, particularly in the information technology sector. The percentage of federal purchases made through multi-vendor contracts is likely to increase dramatically in the future.

End users like multi-vendor contracts because the products or services needed are acquired very quickly. Contracting officers favor multi-vendor contracts because they can buy what end users want expeditiously within the rules, using minimal staff resources, and with less paperwork. Federal contracting organizations are experiencing ever-increasing workloads while losing staff and they could not function without multi-vendor contracts.

Popular Types of Multiple-Vendor Contracts

There are many types of multi-vendor contracts. The two most popular are summarized below.

Government-Wide Acquisition Contracts (GWACs) are used solely for information technology purchases. There are currently approximately 20 GWACs in effect with more and bigger contracts planned for award during the next two years. Approximately $15 to $20 billion is spent annually through GWACs, although precise figures about GWAC award dollars are not available.

Multiple Award Schedule (MAS) contracts are awarded by the General Services Administration (GSA) for a wide range of commercial products and services. MAS contracts are commonly known as "GSA Schedules contracts" and they exist for more than fifty industry sectors, ranging from office supplies to information technology products and services.

The number of vendors holding a contract is unlimited and vendors may submit a proposal at any time. GSA Schedules are particularly appealing to small businesses. Like GWACs, they may be used by any federal agency, and unlike GWACs, by state and local agencies for information technology products and services. Approximately $70 billion dollars are awarded under MAS contracts annually with roughly $20 billion of that for information technology products and services.

Multi-vendor contracts can be awarded by an agency for use within the agency itself, across several selected agencies within a Department (e.g., Department of Defense agencies only) or by any federal agency (as is the case with the GSA Schedule contracts). The dollars spent for this type of contract can be enormous even when used only for a specific agency.

If using a multi-vendor contract, the end user or contracting officer identifies his or her need. Bid requests are then issued to three or more vendors holding the contract in question. The required paperwork is quick and fast, and an order can be processed and filled in several weeks (as opposed to more than two hundred days for a public bid). Under some multi-vendor contracts, the vendor must pay a small fee for the privilege of doing business with the government and to sustain the bureaucracy.

Multi-vendor contracts are used for a wide variety of items and are particularly prevalent for buying information technology products and services. They are used to buy office supplies, military parts and supplies, vehicles, building supplies and recurring services like rental cars. Hundreds of multiple vendor contracts have been awarded by agencies for use by buyers within their own agency (e.g., the Defense Logistics Agency).

This type of contract limits competition and favors the insider. The federal government couldn't function without them and the debate about the competitiveness of this type of contract is centered on how many there should be, not whether they should exist. GSA Schedule contracts are somewhat more competitive than other types of multi-vendor contracts because they are open to all vendors, including small businesses.

The basic types of multi-vendor contracts are summarized below.

Multi-Vendor Contract Comparison

Features/Type	GSA Schedules (MAS Contracts)	Government-wide Acquisition Contracts (GWACs)	Other Multi-vendor Contracts
Requirements are specified at time an order is placed	Yes	Yes	Yes
Approved price lists	Yes	Yes	Yes
Term of contract	5 years plus 3, five-year options	Usually 5 years	3 to 5 years
When vendor proposals are accepted	At any time	Usually a 30- to 60-day window and then contract no longer open	Usually a 30- to 60-day window and then contract is no longer open
Number of vendors	Unlimited (currently 10,000 plus) Note - This makes them attractive to	10 to 40	Varies across agencies

Features/Type	GSA Schedules (MAS Contracts)	Government-wide Acquisition Contracts (GWACs)	Other Multi-vendor Contracts
	small businesses and, in many cases, is their only option.		
Open to small businesses	Yes	Some have small business components	Varies
Number of contracts	50 or more across most industries	15 or more for information technology only	Varies for commodities like office supplies, military material, & information technology
Who is approved to use them	All federal agencies plus over 200 quasi-federal agencies State & local agencies for the information technology schedule only	Any federal agency	One or several federal agencies

The EAGLE and the Alliants

The "eagle" has landed at DHS, so to speak. The Enterprise Acquisition Gateway for Leading Edge (EAGLE) contract is a multi-vendor contract designed to facilitate the procurement of information technology for DHS over a five-year period.

In June 2006, DHS awarded the EAGLE multiple vendor contract to twenty-five large information technology prime contractors, a virtual "who's who" list of federal insiders. EAGLE expenditures are expected to accelerate and could reach $45 billion over the next five years. DHS currently spends roughly $6 billion annually on information technology purchases.

A group of EAGLE contracts set aside for small businesses will be announced in the future. But the number of small companies awarded contracts will represent a tiny fraction of the small companies seeking federal information technology business.

Not to be outdone, GSA announced two additional information technology GWACs in September, 2006. The Alliant and Alliant Small Business contracts are expected to annually spend $5 billion and $1.5 billion, respectively, over the course of the next ten years. When fully implemented, the new DHS and GSA GWACs will represent approximately twenty percent of the total federal information technology contract expenditures. Is there any doubt that GWACs are becoming the procedure of choice for information technology purchases?

Competitiveness of Multi-Vendor Contracts

Multi-vendor contracts limit competition and make purchasing faster and cheaper. The government, when using a multi-vendor contract, need only solicit bids from three vendors holding the type of contract in question. Those not holding such a contract are not considered. The reality is that the bulk of the dollars spent through these programs go to large federal contractors. Most multi-vendor contracts aren't realistically awarded to, or held by, new players in the market.

A GSA Schedule contract is attractive to small businesses because:

- One may be awarded to a business of any size.

- There is no limitation upon the number of vendors that may receive an award of such a contract.

- GSA Schedule contracts are open (meaning that a vendor may submit a proposal at any time and there is no closing date for receipt of such proposals).

Department of Defense (DOD) Contractors Welcome

The federal government opened the Alliant SB GWAC for bids immediately before this book was sent to press. The Alliant SB contract -- a $15 billion multi-vendor procurement -- is a prime example of one of the basic premises in this book; federal procurements that appear to be full and open competitions are open but far from full.

The Alliant SB Request for Proposal requires that those companies submitting proposals have both a security clearance for their facility and an accounting system approved by the Defense Contract Audit Agency. Unfortunately, very few small businesses will be able to meet both requirements. In fact, it is likely that only existing DOD contractors will be able to do so.

Why is GSA demanding such highly-restrictive requirements after patiently listening to the screams of hundreds of small businesses during the public comment stage of the procurement? Because that is what their DOD buyers want and GSA relies on DOD procurement business to stay alive. To summarize: GSA wants what DOD wants.

Although any federal agency can buy information technology services through the Alliant SB contract, the procurement is severely limited in terms of the number of businesses eligible to receive award. As a result, any federal agency (other than DOD) which uses Alliant SB will probably wind up contracting with a small business with DOD contracts.

We estimate that perhaps ten to twenty thousand small IT companies will be interested in bidding on Alliant SB. This group will be narrowed down to several thousand because only companies with average annual revenues of $15 - $25 million will have a realistic chance of meeting the past experience requirements of the procurement. And, as a practical matter, the experience proffered needs to be federal information technology experience (although commercial experience will be considered). In essence, the companies with a good chance of success are those large, small businesses with federal experience.

The two aforementioned DOD requirements narrow the field down further to several hundred potential bidders. GSA will then award perhaps forty contracts. $15 billion for forty companies; you do the math. This is about as far as you can get from full and open competition. The reality is that GSA has done nothing improper in restricting the Alliant SB competition. In fact, given that that it is funded by Industrial Funding Fees, it is in GSA's self interest to cater to DOD, its largest customer by far. GSA needs the fees generated by the Alliant contract to survive.

An Ideal Multiple Vendor Contract

The federal agencies that have developed multi-vendor contract program have not necessarily tackled all of the issues associated with such contracts. An exemplary multi-vendor contract, if one exists, would have the following characteristics:

1. The contract should establish price evaluation policies and related procedures that are fair and reasonable to vendors and the government. This is the essential element of a good multi-vendor contract. The price evaluation policies and procedures must carefully balance the buying power of the government with the right and need for vendors to make a profit. They must also account for fluctuating prices dictated by changing market conditions. The characteristic described above is difficult to achieve. Attempts to make the pricing model fair and reasonable result in complex rules, costly audit requirements, and red tape. The government is often overzealous in its attempt to obtain the lowest possible price and this pursuit frequently results in false economies. Vendors must make a profit to provide quality products and services. When contract prices are set at artificially low rates, there is frequently a corresponding decrease in the quality of products or services provided.

2. The contract should establish a simple procedure for agencies to order products or services from vendors holding the contract. For example, federal buyers may buy products from GSA Schedule holders over GSA Advantage!, the government's electronic shopping mall.

3. The multi-vendor contract should require end users or contracting officers to solicit bids from three or more vendors for each purchase order issued. The contract should further state that if a chosen vendor elects not to compete, the purchasing official must move on to the next vendor until three bids are obtained. In doing so, the government would take a giant step toward ensuring that gets the best possible deal.

In summary, multi-vendor contracts are becoming the gold standard for closing sales in the federal market. They are loved by buyers and sellers because everyone wins, except for those companies which do not have one.

Chapter 6

GSA Schedules

What federal purchasing procedure is open to small businesses and also allows any federal agency to buy virtually any product or service easily?

Only one, a GSA Schedule contract.

Multi-vendor contracts are the preferred way to do business from the perspectives of both buyers and vendors. Since most of the large multi-vendor contracts are won by large businesses, it behooves small and medium-sized businesses wanting to compete for federal prime contracts to get on the GSA Schedule bandwagon.

The Vendor's Perspective

Vendors like GSA Schedule contracts for the same reasons that federal buyers like them. GSA Schedules:

- Reduce competition within the rules

- Allow vendors to avoid a public bid, thereby saving vast sums of money that would have been spent writing a proposal

- Allow vendors to close a deal in a few weeks instead of months

The Federal Buyer's Perspective

As aforementioned, federal buyers prefer to use GSA Schedule contracts because they can:

- Purchase a product by consulting price lists on the GSA Advantage! online database

- Purchase services by issuing an electronic Request for Quote to three GSA Schedule vendors, rather than going through a public bid process

- Use best value considerations in selecting a vendor (using subjective factors like value or service considerations)

You heard it; if you can convince a federal buyer that your product or service is superior to your competitor down the street, federal procurement rules encourage the end user to justify purchases based on "best value" considerations, not necessarily lowest price justifications. GSA Schedules are a federal sales person's dream come true. The biggest problems from a sales perspective are getting in the door and convincing the contracting officer to use a Schedule contract to make the buy. This is where relationship building becomes paramount.

Let's assume that your company is an information technology service business that has sold a web site development project to an end user at a military base in your area. Your company is new to the market and does not have a GSA Schedule contract or a GWAC. For deals that exceed $25,000, your company has only two options. The options are as follows

1. The end user and the contracting officer could arrange for your business to receive a subcontract with one of the base's prime contractors. This solution could be accomplished quickly with minimal, if any, competition, but then you are under the thumb of the prime contractor. The prime contractor will try to reduce your profits so it can take a profit on the subcontract. The prime will also try to minimize your exposure to the customer - - the person to whom you sold in the first place -- as you would if you were in the prime's shoes.

2. The end user and the contracting officer could decide that their only alternative is to publish the requirements for the project as a public bid. This is a less attractive alternative because the public bid will (i) require your company to write an expensive proposal, (ii) expose your business to competition from others interested in the project, and (iii) force you to wait an average of two hundred days or more for an award decision to be made.

Neither of these two options is ideal. A multi-vendor contract would allow you to close the deal in a matter of weeks, as opposed to months, and competition for the project would be reduced significantly. In short, a GSA Schedule contract is the best multi-vendor contract for a small to medium-sized company.

The moral of this story is twofold: Don't get caught without a closing mechanism, and it's never too soon to begin the GSA Schedule application and approval process.

Industries Covered by Schedules

At present, more than fifty general categories of products or services can be sold under the Schedules program. This list includes office products, information technology equipment like computers and software, building supplies, medical equipment, chemical supplies, and a host of professional services such as management consulting and legal, accounting, and professional engineering services.

GSA Schedule contracts are not available for the following industries:

- Research and development

- Architectural and building engineering services. However, there is a Schedule for services in chemical, civil, electrical, and mechanical engineering.

- Construction

GSA Schedule Terms and Conditions

A Schedule contract is a five-year contract containing three, five-year renewal options. In total, if the government were to exercise all three options, the term of the contract would span twenty years. Although a Schedule contract is an official federal contract, it is not funded until orders are placed through the contract. As such, the onus is on the Schedule contract holder to actively solicit orders from federal buyers. Contractors who do not make a minimum of $25,000 in annual Schedule sales run the risk of contract termination.

An "Industrial Funding Fee" funds the Schedules program. Vendors are assessed 0.75% (0.50 % for medical products/services under the VA Schedules) on each dollar sold under their GSA Schedule contract.

Vendors report their Schedule sales to GSA and pay the appropriate funding fee on a quarterly basis.

Getting a GSA Schedule

In order to become a Schedule supplier, a vendor must go through an arduous application process. The Requests for Proposals for Schedule contracts are confusing and difficult to decipher. The process of merely determining which GSA Schedule a company should seek is difficult. A wrong choice can result in rejection of a company's proposal.

Assuming you've selected the correct Schedule, the most problematic and painstaking part of the Schedule application and approval process is negotiating what the Government and vendor agree is a "fair and reasonable price" for the vendor's offered products or services.

GSA's current price evaluation policies and procedures are cumbersome and sometimes unfair because they are based on a vendor's discounting practices rather than the vendor's most recent commercial prices. Discounting practices are often difficult for a vendor to define and the rationale for them can be vague.

GSA Schedule contracts are particularly attractive for small businesses because there is no deadline for submitting an application and an unlimited number of companies may be awarded a contract. Unfortunately for the smaller players in the market, GSA has recently tightened up its qualification and experience requirements. For example, one Schedule Request for Proposal requires that a business be in existenc for a minimum of three years before it will be considered for award. This development has had a direct impact upon the ability of small businesses to win a Schedule contract. Although no one is saying this out loud, smal businesses do not generate sufficient Industrial Funding Fees to fund the GSA bureaucracy.

To overcome the hurdles discussed above, some vendors choose to hire consultants to assist in the preparation and negotiation of the contract. In fact, the difficulties of writing a GSA Schedule proposal have spawned a "we will write it for you" industry in Washington, DC. This can be money well spent as the entire submission and approval process is extremely time-consuming and can be a daunting task for those inexperienced in dealing with the government.

Order Processing

Once a Schedule contract is awarded, the successful vendor is placed on a list of approved suppliers for that particular Schedule. Making a purchase through a Schedule contract is relatively easy.

Federal agency buyers seeking to make a purchase can use GSA Advantage!, the government's online "shopping mall" for GSA Schedule products and services, to see which vendors offer the product or service they need. The federal buyer then sends a Request for Quote to three companies. In response, each company prepares a quote using its approved GSA Schedule contract prices as its pricing basis. The buyer evaluates the quotes, decides which vendor to use, and places a purchase order against the vendor's GSA Schedule contract. The purchase order is then sent directly to the vendor.

The simplicity of the system is illusory, and many vendors, as mentioned previously, are deluded into believing that purchase orders will just roll in once they've obtained a Schedule contract. This expectation is unrealistic. There could be two hundred vendors on a particular Schedule, yet only ten are actually receiving any appreciable federal business. Schedule contract holders must actively sell their company's capabilities to prospective federal buyers. Don't expect business to simply fall in your lap because you have a Schedule contract. It will take focused, agency-based sales efforts. But now you can at least close the deal.

Buyers rave about the efficiency of the GSA Schedule process and the significant reduction in paperwork and red tape associated with Schedule buys. Also, Schedule purchases are transacted behind the scenes without much scrutiny from non-participating vendors. This lack of transparency cuts down on costly vendor protests.

An additional advantage is that virtually any federal buyer can buy from GSA Schedule holders. Congress also granted state and local agencies the authority to make purchases through the Information Technology Schedule contract (known as the "IT 70 Schedule"). State and local purchasing authority may be extended to other GSA Schedules in the future.

Advantages of Schedules

Those hardened veterans who have worked inside the Beltway for an eternity think of GSA Schedules in almost mystical terms because the prices, terms, and conditions of the contract are theoretically negotiated once and then the 200-page tome of specifications collects dust unless brought up by the auditors. Further, they:

- Are the preferred sources of supply for the federal government

- Can be used by all federal agencies and hundreds of non-profits that operate under the public procurement umbrella, like the Red Cross

- Cover most industries (there are currently more than fifty separate schedule contracts)

- Can be used by state and local governments for information technology products and services; Congress is considering extending this privilege across all Schedules

- Can be obtained by small businesses willing to tackle the process of getting a Schedule contract

Another key advantage is that the GSA solicitation for goods or services is always open and a company can submit a proposal at any time. The megabuck multi-vendor contracts, such as the GWACs, differ in that a Request for Proposal is issued with a drop-dead date for submitting a proposal, only a select few are awarded a contract, and the opportunity to bid doesn't come up again until the contract is renewed in five years or so

Drawbacks

GSA Schedule contracts do have drawbacks. Obtaining one can cost in excess of $15,000. The return on this investment is low unless a company has substantial annual Schedule contract sales. Other drawbacks include:

- A Schedule contract reduces a vendor's commercial pricing flexibility and may result in reduced profits.

- Your ability to increase your GSA contract prices is restricted by the terms of the contract.

- The contract's terms require that the vendor carefully monitor and control its commercial discounting practices. Indiscriminate or random spot commercial discounting can lead to automatic reductions in GSA contract prices.

- A GSA Schedule contract may be terminated if a business does not meet the annual sales threshold of $25,000.

Schedule orders must be carefully tracked and accounted for to ensure that the proper Industrial Funding Fee is paid at the end of each quarter.

Drawbacks aside, a GSA Schedule is the selling vehicle of choice for many. An aggressive company willing to devote dollar and staff resources to developing federal business can reap great rewards through its GSA Schedule contract.

Chapter 7

Playing the Federal Sales Game

How do you play a game where the rules are stacked in favor of others? Learn to stack the deck for yourself or don't play.

Playing in the federal market is a game in the same sense that selling in the commercial market is a game. To play successfully you must study the written rules, figure out the unwritten strategies, get burned a few times, and win a few times. This takes time, money, and patience.

Let's assume that you are a commercial company or a start-up and you have decided to enter the federal market. First, you should determine whether your company is willing to make the required investment in a full-time federal salesperson. Then ask yourself if you have the patience to wait a year or more for that salesperson to produce revenue.

Corporate management must understand that it cannot dump a federal sales initiative on an overworked commercial sales staff and expect result Although it is possible for an owner or principal of a small business to handle a company's federal sales program, don't fool yourself into thinking that a significant investment commensurate with your company size isn't required. The person tasked with federal sales cannot dabble part-time in the endeavor and think that results will magically materialize.

When the Sale Takes Place

Almost all newcomers to the federal market make the mistake of thinking that a sales opportunity arises when a request for a proposal or bid is published. In reality by the time a bid is published, the sale has probably already been made. Successful vendors have long-standing relationships with the end users and contracting officers with whom they work, and in many cases help identify problems and solutions before any thought of issuing a contract has arisen.

How many vendors will be selling the same opportunity? It depends on both the size and type of opportunity: The bigger the opportunity, the more vendors will be going after it. Some vendors will have the opportunity on their wish list but will burn out in the proposal-writing phase. Others may want to bid but simply haven't laid enough groundwork to be serious contenders. Others will be dead serious, focused, have a relationship with the end user and the willingness to spend the time and money it takes to win a bid opportunity.

The number of serious contenders depends on the size of the opportunity. Expect to see one or two for a $200,000 opportunity, three to six for a $5 million opportunity, and ten or more for the megabuck contracts, some of which can easily exceed several billion dollars. The bigger the project, the larger the pool of vendors attracted to the opportunity. Gigantic contracts are really only open to the top fifty prime contractors, and they're usually working in teams. For example, the DHS U.S. Visitor and Immigrant Status Indicator Technology (US-VISIT) procurement will probably attract teams from the top ten information technology contractors.

The amount of competition also depends on the risk perceived by the end user; does the government know if there is a practical and economical solution to their problem? The more uncertainty the more likely the procurement will be competitive.

Searching for Sales Opportunities

Products, services, and technology-based solutions are sold through relationships in both the commercial and federal sectors. In the federal arena, relationships are even more important because most federal customers are extremely risk averse - - much more so than in the commercial sector. Except in rare circumstances, companies will not make a federal sale unless a strong relationship has first been established with the customer. This is why it can take a year or more to make a sale in the federal market.

Members of the public see only opportunities that have reached the public bid stage. The uninitiated spend thousands of dollars writing large, complex proposals in response to a Request for Proposal, believing a responsive proposal or ingenious approach to getting a job done will lead to a winning bid. The federal government fosters this perception by creating the illusion that it is actually holding a competition when a public bid is posted. If there is competition, it will be between two or more companies that have established a relationship with the customer well in advance of the bid publication.

This can't be stressed too much. In order to win a public bid opportunity, a company must have pre-sold the opportunity and established a relationship with the federal buyer <u>prior</u> to responding to a Request for Proposal. Of course, exceptions do occur. Rarely, opportunities arise and not a single company has met with the end user. It also sometimes snows in July. Another extremely unlikely but not completely out of the realm of possibility scenario: A company that doesn't have a relationship with the end user writes a creative proposal and prevails over companies with long established relationships.

Buyer-seller relationships are absolutely essential in the federal market and they are nearly impossible to establish without an experienced, full -time sales person in Washington, DC. Establishing relationships is far more important than having the solution itself.

Here's a typical newbie scenario. You think you have the best terrorist tracking software solution known to man and you've identified the person at DHS who will jump when he finds out about it. You plan to go to your congressperson to seek help in raking in those coveted DHS dollars. This is what is likely to happen:

- Your congressperson sends a letter to the DHS that ends up in the circular file.

- The DHS end user won't return your calls.

- After repeated calls, you finally get a meeting with the DHS end user and you spend $1,000 to fly to DC with great hopes.

- In the meeting the end user says: "Looks good, but I have had my prime contractor working on this for over a year and they tell me they have several packages similar to yours. Here's their number. I referred the last ten people with tracking software to them as well. Good luck. Please pass on my regards to your congressperson."

- The prime contractor refuses to return your phone calls.

What's the message here? Find $250,000, hire an experienced full-time sales person, and give them a year to get your first sale.

How early should you identify a sales opportunity in the federal market? Ideally, an opportunity should be identified before anyone, including the customer, knows that an opportunity exists. Companies trying to break into federal sales frequently come to us with the following agenda:

"We don't want potential opportunities. Instead, we want contact information for potential customers who know they have a problem, have approved money to solve the problem, and are ready to contract out to solve the problem."

Although such opportunities exist, everyone selling to the end user knows about them, and in all likelihood your competitors have already sold the customer.

Importance of Direct Sales

Many companies looking to win federal contracts spend large portions of their annual budgets on marketing, business development, and capture planning. Often, these businesses are the very same companies that have not invested in one dedicated federal salesperson. The absence of experienced salespeople is the reason that so many businesses fail in their quest to win government business.

Designations, such as those associated with small disadvantaged businesses or veteran-owned businesses, are not guaranteed to bring in contracts. Federal programs, which set aside millions of dollars for businesses with certain economic and social classifications, are extremely important and needed in the federal marketplace. But federal end users and contracting officers do not seek out these types of businesses. It's up to a company's representatives to directly sell the fact that they have a certain status, like an 8(a) disadvantaged business designation.

Although there are many pitfalls for companies entering the federal arena, none is more costly or prevalent than the mistake of not adequately focusing on the relationship-building aspect of the sales process. Too many companies focus their energies on courting the contracting officer instead of the person within the federal agency who will actually be using their product or service. Once an end user trusts a vendor, the chances for repeat business increase dramatically. The prime government contractors know that relationship sales are the foundation of a successful federal sales campaign.

Direct sales calls and maintaining established relationships also ensure that the end user knows that your product exists. This sounds like Business 101, but you'd be amazed at how often this simple step is overlooked. I hear from dozens of business executives on a weekly basis who ask me, "I have my approved price lists. Where are my government orders?"

End users and contracting officers don't make selections by throwing a dart at a list of approved vendors and buying from the company that the dart lands on. Holding a multi-vendor contract is not an equal opportunity set-up; buying decisions are made based on past track record and information gained from personal interactions. Business goes to the vendors the end user trusts and this means putting in the effort to establish and maintain working relationships with targeted agencies.

Make it Easy

Once you've hired the full-time sales person, made the direct sales calls, established a relationship with the end user, and sold your product or service, you figure you're done, right? No. Vendors need to make it easy for the end user or contracting officer to choose their product or service. Companies make it easy for procurement officials by already having a pre approved selling contract such as a GSA Schedule.

In real estate, they say that success is all about "location, location, location." In federal contracting, it is all about "relationships, relationships, and relationships."

Don't Get Caught without a Closer

Here's an example of how the federal sales game is really played. Let's suppose a federal agency has the money to fund a large information technology project, creating a potential, although as yet unidentified, sale opportunity. Your salesperson calls on the end user. The initial sales contact could have been made through a cold call, through a referral from someone inside or outside the government, or as the result of a relationship developed earlier when the end user was in industry or the salesperson was in government. The stronger the previous relationship or referral the better, but it doesn't really matter how you get through the door as long as you get there.

The salesperson and end user continue to meet, talk on the phone, and communicate via e-mail, discussing the end user's program goals, the challenges to reaching those goals, and possible ways of addressing any problems. The salesperson's goal is to establish a relationship, convince the end user there is a problem, and that your company has the solution. This can take several weeks to a year or more. The salesperson, in an effort to develop and refine a solution, meets with other management and technical specialists within the targeted agency at the same time.

Once everyone has agreed that both a problem and a solution exist, the end user meets with the contracting officer to discuss how the needed product or service is going to be procured. The end user informs the contracting officer of your company's involvement, but realizes, of course, that the procurement must be competitive. However, it is understood that the end user would prefer to work with the company that already understands the problem and has presented a solution. The contracting officer and the end user discuss how the deal will be closed.

Under the scenario discussed above, the first option is for the work to be done under a subcontract with a prime contractor already working for the agency. This would be a quick way to close the deal but presents several problems. The contracting officer is required by law to direct the prime contractor to buy from subcontractors competitively, so your company might not get the work. The government has to pay the prime contractor's overhead, and the prime contractor will reduce your profits so it can take a profit on the subcontract.

In addition, the end user is theoretically supposed to work directly with the prime contractor rather than the subcontractor. Note, I said theoretically. But even if you work with the federal end user directly, you are still under the thumb of the prime contractor.

Alternatively, the end user and the contracting officer could decide that their only option is to publish the requirements for the project as a public bid. Your company will have to write an expensive proposal, you will be exposed to significant competition from others interested in the project, and it will take an average of two hundred days or more for an award decision to be made.

The best solution is to use a multi-vendor contract to close the deal. As mentioned previously, GSA Schedule buys can be accomplished in a matter of weeks, as opposed to months, and competition for the projec is reduced significantly.

The moral of the story: Make it easy for the buyer to choose you. Contracts like the one outlined above usually take six months to a year or more to sell, and obtaining a GSA Schedule contract requires about the same amount of time. Start on your GSA Schedule application now and don't get caught without a closing mechanism when it is time to sign a contract.

The Role of the Contracting Officer

As indicated above, federal contracting officers have far more influence on a purchasing decision than commercial purchasing agents. Contracting officers ensure that buys are made within the rules although the end user usually makes the final purchasing decision. A dialogue concerning a typical federal buy might go like this:

End user to contracting officer: "I have met with an IT company that has the solution to my problem and no one else has what they can offer. I have the $250,000 in my budget to buy their solution. I have a specification that I developed with their help. I am under the gun from above to get this problem solved; can we get them a contract within a week or so?"

Contracting officer: "You have got to be kidding. Let's start with the basics. There are probably a number of companies that can solve your problem. I should have known about this requirement months ago. We can probably get this done in a month or so but you are going to have to get quotes from at least two other companies. You are going to have to play by the rules. Does the company you've been talking to have a GSA Schedule or any other multiple vendor contracts for IT services?"

End user: "I will check but I don' think so. Can't we just go sole source?"

Contracting officer: "No, we can't. It doesn't appear that what the company offers is particularly unique and, even if it were, the process of getting sole-source approval would probably take three to four months. We may be able to tack this on as a subcontract with our prime IT vendor. But I am going to have to insist that the prime vendor get bids from two more companies. Get back to me with an answer to the GSA Schedule question. We can work together to get this done but we have to have competition within the rules."

End user: "I appreciate your help. But my boss is not going to be happy. We need this as soon as possible."

Contracting officer: "Your boss knows the rules. He and I have been through this before. Have him call me if I need to refresh his understanding of the rules."

Marketing

Some believe that marketing is a critical component to having success in the federal market. Marketing efforts make the public, official buyers and end users aware of your company and your products or services. My definition of marketing includes distributing press releases, advertising, participating in conferences and trade shows, conducting seminars, and employing targeted direct mail, e-mail and fax campaigns.

As a general rule, it's unwise to spend big dollars on marketing when first entering the government marketplace. Remember, the key to success in this market is focusing on target agencies. Marketing tends to take you in the opposite direction. Early in the game, your interest in securing contracts should far outweigh your interest in brand identity.

Marketing works best for large government contractors. Why?

- They have more money.

- They have GSA contracts and other contracting vehicles they can advertise to government end users and buyers.

- They need to let other companies know about their capabilities for teaming purposes.

- They like to get together at conferences and share war stories over cocktails and hors d'oeuvres.

In a limited sense, companies market as a natural byproduct of doing business. Examples include sending out a capabilities brochure to target customers, issuing an occasional press release when there is something significant to report, writing articles for publications, going to local networking breakfasts, and attending or sponsoring charity events. That's not what we're talking about here. These forms of cheap marketing can b effective. What we're saying is be cautious about traveling to out-of-state, multi-day conferences or placing $10,000 ads; the money can be better spent elsewhere.

The following marketing activities can work for small to medium-sized businesses:

- Send direct marketing literature to end users and buyers, and follow-up with direct sales calls.

- Conduct your own product or service demo event. This is only effective if you can get buyers and end users to attend.

- Write articles targeted directly to the government audience.

- Issue press releases. They are cheap to do and can be effective especially if they are reprinted in publications read by government end users.

- Consider advertising. Many find advertising to be too expensive until the government profits start rolling in. If you advertise, focus on targeted online and offline publications that government end users actually read.

- Attend government-sponsored vendor conferences. Although the buyers are there, end users don't usually attend. You might make good contacts, but don't count on it. Try to know who is attending before you decide to go. It's best to start with this type of meeting i your immediate geographic area to keep costs down.

- Attend large trade shows for the government market. These can be very expensive. If you must go, see if you can attend under the sponsorship of a prime contractor with whom you work. Share a booth to reduce expenses. Again, it's best to start within your immediate geographic area to keep costs down.

So, have I mentioned the importance of a relationship with the federal end user enough? Overkill maybe, but experienced federal contracting executives often forget this basic principle in their everyday battle for contract revenue.

In summary, learn the rules and play by them. Sell the end user and then work with the end user and contracting officer to find a way within the rules to close your sale.

Chapter 8

Selling Solutions

Which is more important, having a brilliant solution or an established relationship with an end user? Thinking that a top-notch solution will get you into the federal market is a mistake. Everyone thinks their solution is ingenious and sophisticated federal end users roll their eyes when they hear that pitch.

Even being a qualified service business does not cut it in today's federal market. Tens of thousands of companies can claim that they are experienced service companies. Today you have to have an end user relationship first, a customer solution next, and the last and least significant factor is corporate experience.

Sell Risk Aversion

Risk aversion plays a part in purchasing decisions in all industries. Minimizing risk is an even bigger factor for federal buyers for two reasons. First, federal buyers rely on contractors more than their counterparts in the commercial sector; it's not unusual for the bulk of a federal manager's staff to be contract personnel. A federal buyer's entire career (promotions, salary, future opportunities) can depend on a contractor's performance.

To successfully sell in the federal market, you need to find the buyer's comfort zone and eliminate risk as much as possible. You can do this by identifying possible pitfalls in a project and discussing them fully with the buyer, both verbally and in your written proposal. Avoiding or minimizing risk is the primary reason that federal buyers favor incumbent contractors and large prime contractors - - it's a "better the devil you know" kind of mentality.

The press is full of stories about the failure of large, complex information technology and military weapon contracts. Entire books have been written on the lack of oversight, incompetence, and profligate spending involved in Iraq and hurricane reconstruction contracts. Stories like this can negatively affect many careers (although not apparently under the Bush administration). Trust in the federal market really means that the buyer trusts you to minimize his risks and keep him out of trouble.

End users have a great fear of disruption of services. The thought process of a federal Chief Information Officer might be as follows:

"My prime contractor successfully (albeit sloppily at times) runs my network serving 20,000 federal employees worldwide. And now the contracting officer is insisting that I put the next five years of the contract out for public bid; lots of luck to those electing to bid. I will listen to their stories but they better be bullet proof. I would need the following to switch:

- The bidder would need ironclad agreements that key members of the incumbent's staff, especially the project managers, will join them and work on the contract.

- The bidder would have to have a plan to retain all of the incumbent's staff and a foolproof plan for replacements just in case a few decide to leave.

Even with these assurances written eloquently in the proposal, it might not be enough."

Selling Services versus Products

The degree to which a business must develop a relationship with the end user is based on the complexity of a service and its uniqueness. Think of it as a sliding scale of relationship building effort: On the lower end you're selling 10,000 glass beakers; on the upper end, you're selling the computer system that will support the Social Security Administration.

Services are inherently more difficult to sell because they are essentially invisible. A service company must convince the buyer that it understands the buyer's problem and has a practical solution to the problem. Selling services and integrated solutions usually requires lengthy, intense, and costly direct sales efforts. Sales are generally closed using a multiple-vendor contract or a public bid.

Public bids are usually posted in the form of a Request for Proposal. Responding to the Request for Proposal requires that bidders write an extensive and lengthy proposal and then have the hand truck and rented van necessary to deliver the 1,000 to 100,000 pages of proposal material required to paper the government's procurement trail.

In the products market, end users often are familiar with the products they are buying. Did you meet with a Microsoft salesperson before purchasing Microsoft Office? Does Microsoft even have salespeople? Our company bought Oracle software and Sun servers without meeting with salespeople. We learned about the products through word of mouth and Internet research. Fortunately, competition and open-source software have changed the environment that existed back then and even the mighty Microsoft may have to sell its more complex offerings today. Maybe karma really exists.

Although products companies must build relationships, their investment in terms of time and money is not as great as in the services setting. As in the services market, a federal product sale is closed using a multi-vendor contract transaction or a public bid. The public bid is usually posted in the form of a Request for Quote but, in some instances, a Request for Proposal is used.

Responding to a Request for Quote usually does not require a voluminous proposal. Bids can be submitted on hope alone. If you lose the opportunity, use the Request for Quote as your mechanism to interact with the customer. Consider calling the customer afterwards to ask why you were not chosen and then sell him on the great worth of your products.

Scenario of a Technology Sale

The following scenario illustrates a successful, complex solutions sale.

The Chief Information Officer (CIO) of Agency A was formerly employed with Systems Inc., a commercial company specializing in high-end database development. The current Vice President (VP) of Systems Inc. worked with the Agency's CIO while the CIO was at Systems Inc.

The VP has been friendly with a database software sales person for years. The two chat at Northern Virginia Technology Council events and occasionally meet for lunch or drinks.

The Systems Inc. VP calls on Agency A and finds that a large database management requirement exists. Working closely with the Agency's CIO, the Systems Inc. VP creates a proposed solution that involves his company's development services and the friend's software package. The closing mechanism for the sale is a GSA Schedule, with Systems Inc. as the prime contractor, and the database software manufacturer folded in as a subcontractor.

Agency A's CIO likes the database software performance and recommends the software to Agency B. Agency B accordingly buys the software. As time goes on, the two companies continue to work together and the software manufacturer brings the Systems Inc. VP into a deal with Agency C. Under the GSA teaming agreement with Agency C, the software manufacturer is the prime contractor.

And the circle goes on.

Real versus Bureaucratic Requirements

When selling solutions, it's important to recognize the difference between bureaucratic requirements and real needs. You may think you have the answer to the federal government's prayer. But the end user may not perceive the problem in the same light you do. It could be a question of differing priorities; it may be that the government doesn't see a problem, or no one is praying for a solution. The end user might agree with you entirely, but be unable to act because of bureaucratic or legislative mandates.

Suppose that you sell improved satellite communications equipment. You would naturally think that you have an important solution to a pressing problem. And your solution could solve a real problem. But the bureaucracy may be taking the "head in sand" approach and not recognize the problem or have different priorities (such as all available monies are being put into on-the-ground communication systems, for example). The bureaucrats may hope the problem will simply disappear before they have to do anything about it.

Companies can spend years beating their heads against the bureaucratic wall trying to sell their miraculous solution when, in fact, they never had a chance because they were out of step with bureaucratic priorities.

What you need to keep in mind is that thousands of vendors are pounding on the federal market door.

Sell the customer what they want, not necessarily what they need. Sell them what they need through contract modifications if what they want doesn't turn out to be a full solution. The federal buyer and contracting officer are not interested in how marvelous your company is, or how creative your product is; they are interested in themselves and their problem. They will not look to make an innovative choice. They merely want to avoid making a bad one.

Getting Through the Door

Getting through the door of an end user's office to establish relationship requires patience, persistence, and focus. Federal procurement decision makers and end users are expected to be open to meeting with all vendor and are not supposed to show favoritism. At the same time, vendors from countries all around the world are pounding the door, trying to sell their wares.

The most important thing to remember is that end users are people trying to do their job. They are going to be more eager to meet with people who appear to understand their problems and may have solutions. They will figure out a way to avoid meeting with vendors who appear to be on a fishing expedition.

An obvious question is, "How can I know an end user's problems without meeting with them first?" Identifying problems is not easy but it can be done. Use the Internet and phone calls to conduct research on the targeted agency's programs, the structure of the organization, and each individual's job responsibilities. Talk to other vendors, use your networking contacts, and deduce what their problems may be.

Focus on the end users who appear to need you. For instance, a Chief Information Officer responsible for systems using Oracle database software is bound to have problems you can solve if you sell Oracle middleware. Find out what the target's job responsibilities encompass and develop your suggested solutions before you meet with the CIO.

The best contracting opportunities are the ones that are hidden. Why? First, your competitors will be swarming around the ones in plain sight. Second, knowing about an opportunity early gives you more time to develop a deeper understanding of what the end user needs. In fact, if you have a quality product or service, and you've earned some trust, you may even be able to help determine what the end user needs.

Where are the hidden opportunities? Perhaps jotted down in the minutes of a staff meeting or buried deep in the mental "wish list" of a program manager -- any place, really, that represents early contemplation of what agencies plan to acquire. So what does it take to find them? Imagination, patience, and persistence. What are some of the things you'll have to do? Conduct research, make phone calls, and knock on doors. If finding hidden opportunities sounds a bit difficult, that's because it is. But, of course, that's what makes finding them so great.

Trying to Get the Meeting

Keep two issues in mind when trying to get that first meeting. Vendors must (i) understand an end user's business needs, and (ii) offer specific ideas to help solve his problems. Provide the end user with brief highlights of your proposed presentation when you are asking for a meeting. Enter a meeting with specific ideas on how you would solve the end user's issues. Otherwise, the people on both sides of the table are wasting their time.

Relationships in the federal market can be developed in many ways. Practically everyone hates making cold calls, but in many cases it is the only practical way for those new to federal sales. You have a few options beyond cold calls:

- Acquisitions. Larger companies can acquire another federal contractor with existing contracts in agencies where they do not have a presence.

- Industry events. Consider attending industry events such as annual conferences or smaller gatherings hosted by the Industry Advisory Councils, vendor associations, and other organizations. Events are an ideal place to have a first conversation with an end user.

- Recommendations. Vendors who have helped an end user at one agency are often recommended to other end users. The government community can be smaller than people think; end users know each other. They meet and discuss things. If you impress one, you may wind up impressing many.

- Meetings with lower-level agency officials. Your first meeting might not be with the top end user but with deputies, branch chiefs, and other managers. These meetings are often easier to get and they can help you build credibility. In some cases, lower-level officials may be more important than their bosses in making procurement decisions. They are usually on the source selection committee and often their vote can be the key to winning.

- Send e-mail messages. E-mail messages are less intrusive than phone calls and give the end user a chance to absorb your message without feeling an immediate need to respond. But the e-mail message must be provocative and convince the end user that you understand the problem and have creative ideas on a solution.

Should you sell top down or bottom up? Sell in the middle to the end user with a problem or specific requirement. Often, the end user will not have the authority or money to transact a sale. Sell above the end user in the organization but only with the end user's concurrence and support.

Mistakes to Avoid

- You should avoid the following mistakes if you want to make a good impression in the first meeting:

- Don't oversell your capabilities, flex your muscles, or boast. Don't say you have a unique solution or that you are eminently qualified.

- Don't try to strong-arm the end user.

- Don't seem too eager or aggressive.

- Don't pad your message. Highlight your experience and your ideas that might help solve perceived problems, but don't make claims you can't prove or support.

- Don't neglect the customer's needs. Avoid coming across as someone who only wants to sell a canned solution.

In summary, understanding that risk aversion is at the heart of the solutions sales process is crucial. It's why building a customer relationship is so important, why penetrating the federal market requires a major investment, and why the insiders get bigger and bigger. It isn't that federal officials don't want new vendors; it's that they just want to sleep well at night.

Chapter 9

Developing a Federal Sales Program

Now that you understand the reality of federal sales, you may ask, "How do I find the end users I need to sell and develop a federal sales program?" Finding end users can be more of an art than a science. So where should you start?

Develop an End User Call List

Upwards of a million federal employees purchase products and services worldwide. The easiest way to find them is through the Internet. Like wading through red tape, finding procurement decision makers is not difficult, but it requires tenacity and research skills. A recent college graduate with Internet research experience can do it, allowing you to focus your expensive salespeople on making sales calls.

Use the Internet to compile a list of end users who you think may buy your product or service. The following web site is an excellent starting point for Internet research: http://www.lib.lsu.edu/gov/fedgov.html.

Supplement Internet research with other sources. Monitor the federal public bid site, Fedbizopps.gov, to see what contracting officers are buying. You can go to agency procurement forecast web pages at http://www.sba.gov/GC/forecast.html. Also, scrutinize Washington, DC press articles for opportunities. Have your staff attend government-sponsored procurement conferences.

Look for sales opportunities, or the re-bids of existing contracts, in sales databases that are sold as subscription services. Although the opportunities listed are often solid leads, the competition is intense. In the case of re-bids, the incumbent vendors have been selling the customer for the entire duration of their contracts. Once you break into the market, the same will be true for your company if you deliver the goods. Most companies find that their federal sales improve as they gain experience in the federal market.

The critical question is how potential customers can be targeted before your competitors find them. There is no secret formula to developing a federal sales plan--it is just focused research.

Focus Your Research

If it's an art, how do you get started with the research? The first key points of information to identify include the following:

- Agency information

- Organizational data

- Titles and contact data for end users and official buyers

- Historical data on who is buying what product or service

When doing research on the Internet, you need to focus your efforts. Consider the following tips:

- Geographic focus: Small businesses selling commercial products and commodities and small service companies can focus on the agencies in their geographic area.

- Functional: Companies selling training, IT services, recruiting, human resources, etc. can focus first on an agency and then on the people who head related departments within an agency. For example, the companies mentioned in the preceding sentence would want to target the training director, the chief information officer, the head of personnel, etc.

Commercial companies -- such as Fedmarket.com -- compile and refine the data to save you research time and expense. But even the specialists spend a lot of time on research because the ultimate "what they buy" list doesn't exist.

Public Bid Data as a Sales Tool

Public bid and subsequent "awarded to" data provide the best information available for developing a call list. The data is free and can be found on the federal government's public bid web site, FedBizOpps, www.fedbizopps.gov. But as the saying goes, you get what you pay for, and it takes work to take advantage of this free data. Bid and award data are not tied together and buying history data is not available by buyer.

The information on FedBizOpps is limited. When a public bid is posted, the solicitation document contains a summary (or "synopsis") of the scope of work for the project. The complete scope of work is included in the actual contract itself; the only way you'll ever see it is to make a request under the Freedom of Information Act and wait for months. The award document in FedBizOpps shows the date of the contract award, the dollar amount of the contract, and the name and address of the company receiving the contract.

End User Contact Data

Why is it so hard to find end users? The federal government doesn't like to publish end user contact data because it leads to a deluge of vendor phone calls. As aforementioned, Congress recognizes the need for a more open federal market and has enacted legislation to create a public, online database of contract award data (including information on what was purchased and end user information for each contract). This would be a grand step forward, but I would not count on it happening any time soon.

At present, you have to find out who the end users are by word of mouth, telephone research, Internet research, or by looking at organizational charts and directories. Keep in mind that there can be more than one federal official responsible for making purchasing decisions for a large buy. Often, you have to surmise who the end user is by their title. A Human Resources Manager probably buys recruiting services or software, for instance.

Contracting officers know who the end users are but may be reluctant to tell you. A typical conversation with a contracting officer might go like this:

Vendor: "I see from my research that you awarded a contract on May 11, 2005 for $500,000 worth of network routers to Acme Reseller. Who was the end user in your information technology organization?"

Possible Answer: "John Brown is at this telephone number and his e-mail address is ......"

More Probable Answer: "I don't really know and I would have to dig out the contract to find out."

Vendor: "I would appreciate it if you would do that and call me back."

Contracting officer: "I'll try but I can't promise you anything due to our overwhelming workload in this office." (Translated: Don't sit by the phone.)

Vendor: "I read a book on federal sales and it said that the contracting officer is the single point of contact for the vendor community."

Contracting officer: "You are correct, but as I remember the end user already had brand name routers and just wanted some more. They really don't want a ton of vendor calls."

The issue of whether the contracting officer is legally required to give out an end user's name is gray. You have the legal right to request a copy of the contract itself under the Freedom of Information Act (FOIA) and then wait anywhere from one to twelve months for a response. By the time you get the contract, the end user will have ordered another large batch of the same network routers. Yes, federal officials violate the twenty-day response time in the FOIA law as a routine matter.

Alternatively, you can do the practical thing and either beg the contracting officer to help you or call the targeted agency's information technology office and ask them for the name of the end user. You may get the run-around there as well. Who ever said that making sales is easy? The bottom line is federal buyers have all the cards so you have to find a way to play their game. Trying to force them to give you contact data is counterproductive.

What do you do when contracting officers stonewall and won't provide the name of an end user? Use keyword searching and select the large awards from the FedBizOpps web site that represent what you sell and appear to be practical opportunities for you if the agency in question is likely to repurchase the same thing. Contracting officers will usually tell you who won a contract and the contract number when an award document cannot be found in FedBizOpps to match the solicitation that you are interested in.

Be very selective about making FOIA requests. The contract may not arrive in time to be useful to you, and contracting officers can become annoyed with FOIA requests. You don't want to annoy those to whom you will be selling.

The federal government has more than a thousand buying organizations. At the very least, use solicitation and award data at FedBizOpps to narrow the list of agencies that you want to target. Then go on the Internet to look at organizational charts, directories, and program descriptions to find end users for the targeted agencies.

Sell Using Your Sales Plan

Once you have contact data, you should begin making federal sales calls immediately. Assign federal sales to one of your salespersons or hire a new person. Find someone with federal sales experience if you fill the position with a new hire. Although difficult, hiring a person with federal sales experience will produce revenue more quickly. You will need to train a salesperson if you cannot find an experienced individual. Federal sales training courses are available in Washington, DC, including those offered at Fedmarket.com.

You ask: "How can we start direct federal sales immediately if we do not have an experienced federal salesperson?" Have an owner, a principal, or your commercial sales manager start making federal sales calls. This may be distasteful to an owner but someone has to do it. The same rejection occurs when making cold sales calls to federal customers as it does when calling upon commercial customers. In fact, the sales process is identical in both markets. The federal market is just bigger and requires more intense focus. On a positive note, the federal customer may be a bit nicer when throwing up the roadblocks to meeting with you. Way down deep they do know that it is a taxpayer who is calling.

Subcontracting

Some companies try an indirect route to federal sales by offering their services to federal prime contractors as an alternative to direct federal sales with the government. The reason most often given for taking a subcontracting approach is that even though direct contracts might mean more revenue, they also mean more red tape and the potential for federal audits. Although the potential for both is real, many companies new to the market give these nuisances too much weight.

The subcontracting approach should be a short-term one and a direct federal sales push should start immediately upon making the decision to enter the federal market. It is as difficult to sell prime contractors, as it is federal end users. Prime contractors usually won't let you through the door unless you're walking in with federal business and the end user has suggested that you use a prime contractor to transact your sale. Invariably, prime contractors will try to keep you on a leash and as far away from the end user as possible.

Preference Programs

The federal government is awash in small business preference programs. Such programs include set asides for small businesses, small disadvantaged businesses, veteran-owned small businesses, women-owned small businesses and others. These are all laudable programs that assist small businesses in obtaining federal business. Most often the edge that the programs provide is a reduction in, not an elimination of, competition.

From a sales perspective, the big danger with these programs is that they can deceive a business into thinking that the set aside alone will produce sales. They won't. Further, don't assume that federal employees really favor small businesses. They don't. They want the company that will reduce their risk and most often that is a large business or the incumbent contractor.

Every business that qualifies should take advantage of the government's small business programs. Some programs allow businesses to self certify their status while others require that an application be filed with the appropriate agency (such as the SBA's 8(a) certification process). Use them to set yourself apart, but view them as an edge as you sell rather than a direct path to a contract. Relying on them is unrealistic.

Administrative Steps

Selling should be your highest priority task. The following administrative steps should be started in parallel on day one.

1. Obtain a GSA Schedule

Start the work required to obtain a GSA Schedule contract on Day One. The big difference between the federal and commercial markets is that you must have a closing mechanism in the federal market because federal procurement regulations require that public money be spent wisely, and that awards occur only after a competition has been held (at least from a public perception). Such contracts are the only effective way for companies new to the market to compete for federal prime contracts.

2. Learn How Federal Proposals Are Written and Develop a Proposal-Writing Capability (Applicable to Professional Service and Information Technology Companies)

Professional services and information technology companies have a unique problem in the federal market. They have to respond to complex, publicly-announced Requests for Proposals even if they have established a strong relationship with the customer. In order to close your sale, you must submit a strong, customer-centric proposal.

Proposal writing can be an Achilles heel for many companies -- even those experienced in the federal market. It is a unique and often chaotic process that is far more expensive and difficult to tackle than most people realize. Writing a winning federal proposal is creative and, at the same time, requires a structured management process. The management process must be systematic and integrate sales and proposal development. The creative part is in selling the customer and then writing the solution that you pre-sold in a way that it is clearly understood by the customer. Both are difficult tasks.

3. Assign an Administrative Person to Complete Red Tape Processes (Jumping through the Hoops)

As discussed above, federal procurement red tape can be a psychological deterrent to direct federal sales. It shouldn't be, however. A newly-hired college graduate with patience or someone in your accounting organization can get through all of the processes necessary to do business with the government. It seems daunting at first but with patience and tenacity the person assigned the task will find out that it is not rocket science. Red tape becomes second nature after the first time through the process.

The designated person should take the following initial administrative steps on Day One. Although mechanical and frustrating at first, taking these steps will help to familiarize you with the federal bureaucracy. Keep in mind that conquering red tape is not sales. It is merely a matter of jumping through hoops. It has nothing whatsoever to do with generating revenue. Outsiders often misunderstand this. Critical steps to undertake are as follows:

1. Obtain a Dun & Bradstreet Number (DUNS Number) (See http://www.dnb.com/US/duns_update/index.html).

2. Register at the federal Central Contractor Registration site (See http://www.ccr.gov/).

3. Register at the Online Representations and Certifications Application (ORCA) site (See https://orca.bpn.gov/login.aspx).

4. Sign up to receive e-mails about federal opportunities at the central Federal Business Opportunities site (See http://www.fedbizopps.gov/).

Do companies need to enlist the services of an attorney when they do business in the federal market? Lawyers have a role to play in the federal market just as they do in the commercial market. The trick is to realize when you need one and when you don't. Don't assume you need one for every little thing you don't understand.

Are special accounting systems required when doing business with the federal government? Yes, at some point but not in the beginning. A somewhat generalized accounting package, such as QuikBooks, will do to start. As your involvement in the federal market grows and your revenue increases, you will need to invest in a specialized system.

In summary, we receive frequent inquiries from companies who tell us they have addressed all of the administrative tasks listed on federal web sites but have failed to receive any federal business. They ask why the orders aren't flowing in from various federal agencies. Our response to such inquiries is to be proactive, locate an end user and call them just like you would a commercial customer. The federal buyers aren't actively seeking you out. Decide to make the investment in establishing one-on-one customer relationships or don't waste your money, time and effort.

Chapter 10

Government Relations and Politics

The massive size of the federal government gives the impression that it is an impenetrable bureaucracy. Yet at its core, federal contracting is a people-to-people business. Successful federal contractors work with their counterparts in the federal government as partners. They perform the work specified in the contract and help federal end users get their jobs done. When contract compliance or performance problems occur, successful contractors inform both their contracting officers and the end user of the problem immediately and work out a solution together as business partners.

Waste, Fraud, Abuse

The problems of wasteful spending, contract abuse and downright fraud in federal contracting have received a lot of press in the wake of the Hurricane Katrina relief efforts and the failure of reconstruction efforts in Iraq. The need for a speedy response and the amount of money in play can quickly corrupt the procurement process.

A recent Congressional report found that DHS wasted billions of contract dollars in the Hurricane Katrina recovery effort. Roughly seventy percent of the federal contracts signed for Katrina recovery efforts were awarded on a no-bid or limited-competition basis. The report found that the issuance of billions of dollars in no-bid contracts, combined with inadequate contract management and oversight, led to pervasive overcharging, wasteful spending, fraud, cronyism, and bribery in Katrina-related contracts.

The reconstruction efforts in Iraq are another case in point. A report by the Special Inspector General for Iraqi Reconstruction (SIGIR) concluded that the Coalition Provisional Authority could not track over $8 billion it had transferred to Iraqi ministries. Numerous other SIGIR reports have documented a range of procurement problems, including excessive reliance on sole-source contracts, instances of outright contractor fraud, insufficient ability to trace the disposition of funds, repeated instances of unsupported contractor costs, and widespread deficiencies in contract oversight.

The bottom line is that people are involved and power and money can corrupt both sides of the process. The government-wide shortage of trained federal contracting personnel to ensure competition and oversee contractor performance needs to be addressed.

Politics and Procurement

Politics can influence who gets contract dollars but not as often as one thinks. Politics come into play when the contract dollars at stake are huge. The federal government's handling of the Katrina disaster was an obvious debacle. Yet, when contracting officials tried to buy material as quickly as possible, they were pilloried by the press and Congress for using sole-source contacts. The needed material or services would have been delivered about the time the next hurricane season hit if they had put the work out for public bid.

It is true that contracting officers can't win in emergency situations. In such situations, the government needs services and supplies immediately and the commercial companies are ready to pounce. Some are in the emergency support game merely for windfall profits and others are experienced federal contractors just trying to make a big profit by responding quickly at increased prices. Making a better profit in time of high demand is the American way but there is a limit. Most reputable federal contractors know where the line is but some have crossed it.

Single-source buys made with Alaskan Native Corporations (ANCs) are frequently criticized by the press and congressional representatives. The buyers are trying to buy efficiently using a quick and entirely legal procedure. Despite widely-reported abuses, ANCs continue to hold special contracting privileges because the state's senator, Ted Stevens, holds a powerful position in the Senate and not because the practice is in the best interests of the taxpayer.

The Executive Branch and Congress enthusiastically and publicly support contracting with small businesses. But try to get real help when it involves an actual purchase. You might get help if you have hired a lobbyist, are a super-sized campaign contributor, or can deliver a truckload of votes. Ask a small business advocate in the federal government to introduce you to a buyer and you're likely to be politely shown to the door. The government's small business advocates say their job is to support small business in general but they really can't favor an individual business.

Can Your Congressional Representative Help?

Making direct sales calls, particularly cold calls, is a chore for most people. Only the exceptionally extroverted salesperson says, "Give me some names and numbers -- I thrive on rejection." Salespersons frequently inquire about alternatives to the cold call. They say, "Why can't I just call my congressional office and ask for help in winning federal business?" You can make those calls but don't expect much. Politicians cannot afford to be concerned about small- to medium-sized businesses except in special situations. They prefer to focus their attention on winning votes and getting campaign contributions from large donors. When will your congressional representative help?

- If your company is bidding on a large project (i.e., the size of the Hoover Dam) in his (and your) district and there are a number of vendors bidding on the project from outside your district.

- If your corporate campaign contributions are so generous that the congressional representative knows your company's name.

- When your business has already won an award and your congressperson wants to take credit for the victory. In this case, your representative will schedule a small business assistance conference in your district, invite a couple of federal buyers, and feature your company as the small business of the year.

Keep in mind that a congressperson cannot help every small business in his or her district. There's not enough time in the day to do so. So don't get discouraged if your efforts to solicit assistance from your congressional representative aren't successful.

Have you received a call from your congressional office honoring you with an appointment to a Blue Ribbon Panel of Outstanding Businessmen? I was honored when I received this call and slightly deflated when I learned that it required a $1,000 campaign contribution. The second time it happened I asked the caller if they had checked the no-call list that Congress helped to create. The person at the other end said: "Give me a break; I'm just a hired telemarketer."

Can K Street Help?

The national news is full of articles about campaign contributions or other favors to obtain "earmarks" - - usually a specific line item inserted into an appropriations bill by a member of congress to support a local project in his or her district. Earmarked funds (i) typically support highway spending and other projects such as the construction of courthouses or prisons, and (ii) are commonly labeled "pork barrel projects" and are awarded without hearings or competition.

Citizens Against Public Waste publishes an annual list of pork barrel projects. The *2005 Pig Book* identified 13,997 projects in the federal budget for fiscal 2005, costing taxpayers $27.3 billion. They have become common on Capitol Hill and increasingly controversial. Federal investigators have been probing whether there are relationships between some earmarks, campaign contributions, and payments to "K Street" lobbyists hired to help obtain federal contracts.

The use of lobbyists to help obtain federal contracts has always been a somewhat controversial approach although it is legal if there are no campaign contributions or favors involved. Doing so costs big bucks and its effectiveness is limited to special situations or exceptionally large projects.

Even powerful legislators on appropriations committees have limited (if any) influence over a procurement decision because end users and contracting officers resent congressional pressure, as they should. Many lobbyists predict that the furor generated by the Jack Abramoff case will soon die down. However, now is probably not a good time to try the lobbyist approach to increase your federal sales.

Can the Revolving Door Help?

In the federal sector, the term "revolving door" refers to the practice of federal employees moving to the private sector and private sector employees moving to federal employment. Some call it the "hire the ex-general" syndrome. Federal employees moving into the private sector can work as full-time employees, consultants, or board members, and can help companies win federal contracts. Such employees can help companies establish relationships with federal end users and can be effective in reducing the need for cold calls. They can also contribute in the sales and proposal-writing process. The practice is perfectly legal as long as the former federal employee does not work directly with their former agency for a period of one year.

The downsides of using former federal employees to help win contracts are (i) it can be a very expensive way to sell, and (ii) it is inherently difficult to measure whether or not the former federal employee really helped or is just blowing smoke about the strength of their federal relationships.

What about Power Brokers?

Press Release: Former Cabinet level official forms consulting firm to assist companies with deep pockets to form new federal relationships. Power Broker Associates announced today that it has added 50 of the Fortune 500 companies to its already impressive list of clients.

Reality: Please write a retainer check to Power Broker Associates. We can get you a meeting with federal officials with money for money.

This is legal. It can help a company get in the door. But that's it and it is definitely an expensive process.

Top Down or Bottom Up?

Some companies try to use their connections with top officials to influence procurement decisions. We call this a "top-down approach" to selling. It doesn't work any better than the congressional approach. Not only is a top-down approach expensive, it can lull you into believing that something is happening and divert you from what you really should be doing. Further, pressure from the top can alienate the mid-level procurement decision makers. Leave the top-down approach for the multi-billion dollar deals and to companies with strong political connections.

Well, you ask, what about a bottom-up approach. Most federal sales are made from the bottom up, or better yet, from the middle up. The person you are seeking is usually a mid-level manager type who is either hiding from you or already has a favorite vendor. It could be an engineer, technical specialist, program specialist, branch chief, division head, or program manager with both a need and money. Finding the end user and then getting through the glass wall - - the resistance to sales calls -- is not easy but it is what you have to do.

Relationships after Contract Award

So after much sweat and blood you have penetrated the market and received a contract award. You may think your relationship-building days are behind you. Think again. Your relationships with end users and contracting officers will dictate future success or failure, and powerfully impact your chances for repeat business (the bread and butter of federal contracting).

Many companies outside the federal market believe that the government can be heavy-handed when dealing with vendors. In fact, most end users are looking for partners, and want as much help as they can get. Any type of adversarial relationship usually ends up with you on the losing end. Like most people, federal managers hate being wrong -- it affects their career file. For the most part, they just want to do a good job, avoid problems and go home to their kids' soccer games. So don't create headaches for them.

Follow these basic rules:

1. Know who holds the cards and play the game the fed's way. They hold all fifty-two cards and the Joker.

2. Perform well and the business will roll in. End users and contracting officers love no-hassle performers and will cut them a lot of slack.

3. Doing a good job seems obvious, but it is really the secret to growth in the market.

4. Don't cut corners, do anything gray, lie, cheat, steal or knowingly certify incorrectly. Do any of these things and federal officials will pound you. If you are wondering about a decision or a practice, or have to ask, don't do it. Down deep you already know the answer.

5. Don't buy gifts or meals for federal officials.

6. Help the end user do their job and be their partner. In fact, think of your staff and the end user as one team trying to the best for the American taxpayer.

7. As the saying goes in ballroom dancing, just follow and you will end up being the leader.

In the old days, the lowest price usually won. New procurement rules now stress value-based purchasing decisions rather than price-based ones. Both procurement experts and vendors sometimes question whether federal contracting officers recognize the need for contractors to make a profit and an adequate return on investment. For the most part, contracting officers recognize value and the importance of profits. If anything, the profits of some contractors may have swung too far in the other direction because of the lack of federal contracting staff to oversee contract performance and compliance.

Don't Be an Adversary

Try not to take an adversarial position with a contracting officer. Don't file a legal protest if you think you have been wronged in a procurement decision. You probably haven't been wronged and you are just feeling the sting of defeat in losing a public bid. Even if you have been wronged, you will end up with a moral victory at the very best and zero future business with the agency. Personally, I would rather have revenue dollars than a moral victory.

If you feel strongly that an unfair decision was made, and you just can't help yourself and feel you must file a legal challenge, do it in writing the minute you determine that procurement rules and procedures are being ignored or broken. If you're right, it's the contracting officer's job to correct the mistake. Try not to whine about issues that are within the rules, like:

-   Objecting to a contract that was awarded with less than full and open competition

-   Challenging a best-value decision or an award based on something other than the lowest price

- Appealing a contract award to a bottom-dwelling competitor of yours

Another tactic unlikely to produce desired results is pointing out to a contracting officer that the agency in question is not meeting their preference goals and that you would be glad to help remedy the situation by signing a contract. Preference goals are just that, goals. Contracting officers like to take a shot at meeting them but no one's salary is docked if the goals to use are not met. At the very most, there will be some wringing of hands, and then the shortfall will go over the dam just like it did last year. Do you tell the interviewer that he has egg on his tie when you are interviewing for a job?

Current Federal Contracting Goals for Certain Small Businesses	
Women-Owned Business (WOSB)	8%
Veteran-Owned Small Business (VOSB)	3%
Service Disabled Veteran-Owned Small Business (SDVOSB)	3%

I can't tell you how many phone calls I've received from business owners and salesmen who say: "Contracting Officer Smith has been buying my competitors' schlock product for years and at a higher price than my superior product. I've had enough; I'm going over his head to fix this problem once and for all."

My response: "Yeah right, good luck. You will not do any business with the agency if you attempt to beat him up."

Another favorite discussion is: "I took the contract to my lawyer (who ha no government experience) and he said we can't sign it without significan changes. Do you think they will meet my terms and conditions?" Short answer: "No, they will go to the next vendor in line."

Federal contracting officers do listen to terms and conditions arguments, but rarely deviate from their standard contracts because they don't have to. They are particularly unresponsive when it comes to revising minor terms or conditions that minimize the vendor's risk.

Corporate ego of any type is almost always counterproductive in the federal market. "We are known for our excellence" and the "the collective experience of our staff exceeds two hundred years" are bragging points sure to draw giggles from federal evaluators reading vendor proposals. Federal buyers are looking for solutions, not sales pitches, and they know the difference between the two.

They are Not Always Right

Almost every federal contracting officer with whom I have dealt has been fair and reasonable and has wielded his power well. Come to think of it, I forgot one. I submitted a large proposal electronically several years ago. I remember thinking that this particular contracting office was on the cutting edge by allowing e-mail proposal submittals. The proposal was due over the Christmas break. As seasoned veterans of contracting battles know, the bureaucracy nearly shuts down over the holidays.

This particular contracting officer was unavailable during his Christmas vacation and furthermore failed to give access to his computer to one of his colleagues. Those venders, including my company, which submitted electronic proposals sat anxiously awaiting an e-mail verification of receipt. No such verifications were forthcoming. Panic ensued because of the government's strict adherence to proposal deadlines. Calls were made to everyone including the contracting officer's boss. But no one could get into his computer.

The contracting officer returned from his vacation and was not pleased that anyone would have the audacity to call his boss concerning whether their $25,000 proposal was received. His solution: "Henceforth this office in no longer going to receive electronic proposals." What a forward thinking solution to a pesky problem and he came up with it all by himself. Quoting Dave Barry, this is a true story.

Formal Protests of Contract Awards

This book will say very little about the risks and benefits of formally protesting contract awards. The bureaucracy does not like to be proven wrong and it will fight until death to prove that it was right.

Approximately ten percent of all protests are successful and only after much time and expense on the part of the protestor and the government.

More importantly, protesting can have a negative impact upon future sale because agencies do not like doing business with sore losers.

The author's personal philosophy on formal protests is that you shouldn' do so unless (i) you can get three experienced government contract lawyers to agree that you have been egregiously harmed, (ii) the lawyers can provide irrefutable evidence of the transgression, and (iii) you can show concrete evidence of the damages you suffered. Also, make sure the attorneys will take the case on a contingency basis. Lastly, expect to become a pariah within the agency against which you have filed the protest.

Debriefings When You Lose

Here is what you do when you lose. Swallow your wounded corporate pride and always ask for a debriefing if you are not selected for contract award. Debriefings are free and you can learn a lot about how to improve your proposals. The government will tell you about your proposal's strengths and weaknesses, but not why the winner won. And there is a big difference. They won't say:

"We really always wanted the incumbent back but were forced into a public bid for appearances."

"A senior person who was employed by our agency is now with the winner and he was able to give them unique insights into our problems."

"The winner outsold you in the requirements definition phase."

"We have known the winner for years and trust them to do a good job."

The real reason for requesting a debriefing is future sales. You will have a chance to meet the end users and tell them about your company. You can show the end user and the contracting officer that you are a good sport and would be an excellent business partner for them in the future.

You can even discuss possible future contract opportunities and when they may be coming down the pike. Most importantly, they will remember you when you call to meet with them about future opportunities. You will create that edge you need when making sales calls and your call will no longer be "cold." They will probably say, "Yes, that was the company tha was so pleasant in the debriefing and didn't press us on why we made the award to someone else. They know how to bite their tongue and play the game and maybe I should quit dodging their calls."

Associations representing federal contractors have denounced an Acquisition Advisory Panel's recommendation to allow a company holding a multiple vendor contract to protest an award to another contract holder. I agree with the industry association's position. This would be akin to encouraging animals feeding on a carcass to feed on each other; clearly a waste of precious government procurement personnel's time and taxpayers dollars. Let's just recognize reality and not let one fat cat holding a multiple vendor contract fight with another at the taxpayers' expense when one outsells the other.

Communication after Contract Award

The key to successful government relations after award of a contract is communication. It's that simple. The contracting officer is the government's legal representative for the contract. You must communicate each and every legal, financial, and performance problem or issue with this person immediately upon encountering the problem; the quicker the better. Contracting officers want to work with contractors to resolve problems early; they know some issues are almost certain to come up and many are beyond the contractor's control. A contractor's willingness and ability to deal with contract issues are demonstrated by early and honest communication. Delayed communication or that which is less than forthright signals exactly the opposite.

Either a project officer (PO) or contracting officer's official representative (COTR) is the person designated to monitor contact performance. The terms are used interchangeably and the designated person is normally from the end user's office. The name of the PO or COTR should be stated in the contact. A PO or COTR scrutinizes the contractor's performance on a day-to-day basis and approves contract invoices. In other words, the PO or COTR shares the governance of contracts with the contracting officer.

The PO or COTR works with the contractor on a daily basis and may have informal knowledge of problems or issues as they arise. However, immediate and formal notification of an issue must be made to the contracting officer because he or she is acting as the legal representative of the government and is therefore the proper party to whom any notice should be given. In the alternative, the issue may be communicated to both parties at the same time.

As an example, suppose that your contract manager (usually designated as a key person in the contract) quits suddenly for whatever reason. This is something that could be considered beyond your control. The PO or COTR and the contracting officer should be contacted immediately and the phone call should be followed by an e-mail or letter. More importantly, you should be prepared, in your initial phone call and subsequent communications, to provide an immediate solution to the problem created by the contract manager's departure.

Communication with the government customer should be done using good management principles. Some might say that in the world of government contracting, the government is your boss. This topic is the subject of a long-standing legal debate but suffice it to say that you can't go wrong if you take this position.

In summary, work with end users and contracting officers as partners, no adversaries. Contracting officers have an unusual amount of power over contractors because of their buying power, immense legal and financial resources, and lack of concern over protests or legal action. Effective contracting officers know their power and do not use it except in cases of significant performance, legal, or financial problems. Generally, they will work with vendors as partners rather than adversaries to resolve problem without wielding their big stick.

Chapter 11

Small Businesses and Federal Sales

The federal government sends small businesses mixed messages concerning their participation in the federal market. From a political standpoint, Congress and the Executive Branch want small businesses to win federal contracts. From an agency standpoint, federal buyers don't have anything against small businesses but three factors tend to make it difficult for small businesses to win federal business. First, end users favor the bigger, well-known insiders because they minimize their risk. Second, contract bundling (combining scopes of work into one large contract) is hurting small businesses. Third, most multi-vendor contracts favor large contractors. The downside can be summed up in three words: "It's a struggle."

On the other hand, small businesses which find success in the federal market have the unique opportunity to grow from a point of little or no revenue to hundreds of millions of dollars of revenue in a few short years. Why? Provided a small business plays on the government's terms, its potential for success is virtually limitless. The federal government encourages small business participation in the market through a series of preference programs. Preference programs work, just not as well as small businesses would like. Even with such programs in place, it is a struggle for small businesses to enter the market. This is particularly true if the businesses can only participate under the regular small business set-aside programs and can't be certified under the more powerful disadvantaged business programs that allow sole source buys.

Preference Programs

The bureaucracy is aware of the insider edge so it created small business preference programs. These programs cover small businesses in general and also specific types of disadvantaged small businesses. The number of preference programs has grown over the years and they work well. Such programs include set asides for small businesses, small disadvantaged businesses, veteran-owned small businesses, women-owned small businesses and others. The preference programs can be confusing to outsiders but they be effective if used in conjunction with a direct sales program. Most often the edge that the programs provide is a reduction i not an elimination of, competition.

The danger associated with these programs is, from a sales perspective, that they lull the small business owner into believing the programs produce business and that direct sales efforts aren't necessary. This is a fallacy. Furthermore, business owners should not assume that federal employees really favor small businesses. They don't. They want the company that will reduce their risk and, as mentioned previously, most often this is a large business or the incumbent contractor.

Every business that qualifies should most definitely use the small busines programs. Some require only a simple "self-certification" while others require the submittal of time consuming and expensive applications to th agency overseeing that program. Take advantage of the small business se aside programs but view them as a closing mechanism, rather than a dire path to a contract. Relying on them solely is unrealistic.

The preference programs are summarized below.

Small Business Type	Annual Contract Dollars in Billions (FY 2005)	Certification Requirement	Competition Rules
Any small business	$79.6	Self-certified. Small business size standards are based on the company's annual revenue or its number of employees (differs by industry classification). Size standards are published by the SBA (http://www.sba.gov/si ze/sizetable2002.html).	All procurements under $ 100,000 are set aside for small businesses Open competitively to any small business that qualify according to the size standards
Small Disadvantaged	$10.5 (includes	An application for certification must be	Sole-source contracting permitted up to the

Small Business Type	Annual Contract Dollars in Billions (FY 2005)	Certification Requirement	Competition Rules
Business	Alaskan Native corporations)	approved by the SBA. Per federal regulations, 51% of the business must owned by disadvantaged individuals.	following limits: $5,000,000 for a procurement within the North American Industry Classification System (NAICS) codes for manufacturing; and $3,000,000 for a requirement within any other NAICS code
Alaskan Native Corporation	(see above)	Applicants certified by SBA	Uncontested sole source awards of any amount allowed
Service-disabled Veteran-Owned Small Business	$1.9	Self-certification but disability certificate required from the Veterans Administration	Same as disadvantaged business (see above)
Business located in a Historically Underutilized Business Zone (HUBZone)	$6.1	Principal office must be, among other criteria, within defined HUB Zones Certification required by SBA based on criteria specified in federal regulations Application for certification sent to SBA	Same as disadvantaged business (see above)
Women-owned Small Business (preference program in the developmental stage)	$10.5	Proposed requirements: 51% owned by women (applies only in industries designated by SBA as substantially underrepresented in federal procurement) 51 % owned by women who are economically	Proposed competition rules: Same as disadvantaged business (see above)

Small Business Type	Annual Contract Dollars in Billions (FY 2005)	Certification Requirement	Competition Rules
		disadvantaged (applies only in industries designated by SBA as underrepresented in federal procurement)	

Under the preference programs discussed above, the contracting officer has the prerogative of sending the opportunity out to more businesses than required under the rules. For example, applicable federal procurement rules may permit a contracting officer to sole source a contract to a small disadvantaged business but he or she may elect to allow a number of businesses to participate in the bidding. Most don't do so because a majority of the contracting offices are understaffed, additional competition is not required, and it creates more work and elapsed time.

The Crown Jewel of the Preference Programs – Alaskan Native Corporations

We briefly discussed Alaskan Native Corporations (ANCs) in a previous chapter. They sit on the top of the pyramid of various preference programs. ANCs receive most of the dollars under the program although the preference legislation also includes Indian tribes and certain community development corporations. These entities are allowed to receive contracts on a sole-source basis without any limitations on the dollars involved. Furthermore, an award to one of these entities cannot be contested. ANCs are also permitted to form subsidiaries to offer different products and services without being subjected to rules that would limit their eligibility if they were privately owned.

New Women-owned Preference Program

Congress enacted new legislation in 2000 authorizing a new small business preference program for women-owned businesses. Nearly six years have elapsed and we are still waiting on the women-owned small business preference program.

The new program will most likely be modeled on the current small disadvantaged business program, the 8(a) Program. We anticipate that the women-owned small business program will be called the 8(m) Program in honor of the section number of the authorizing legislation. This program will allow contracting officers to make sole-source awards to certified women-owned small businesses with the same limitations as several other small business preference programs.

As usual, the government has made the 8(m) Program much more complex and complicated than it should be. It applies only to two specific industry groups and the eligibility requirements for women-owned small businesses are different for the two industry groups. To make matters worse, the industry groups will not be known until SBA completes a study to determine the industry groups. Specifically, SBA is to determine the industries in which women-owned small businesses are "underrepresented" and "substantially underrepresented" in federal procurement.

A summary of the regulations is presented below.

Type of Business	Certification Requirements	Competition May Be Restricted in Specific Industry Groups
Women Owned Small Business	Must be at least 51% owned by one or more women	Industries in which Women Owned Small Businesses are substantially underrepresented in federal procurement
Economically Disadvantaged Women Owned Small Business	Must be at least 51% owned by one or more women who are economically disadvantaged. In order to be considered economically disadvantaged, a woman's personal net worth must be less than $750,000, excluding her ownership interest in the concern and equity in her primary personal residence.	Industries in which Women Owned Small Businesses are underrepresented in federal procurement

Although well intentioned, Congress seems to work at creating confusion. Normal women-owned small businesses and those that meet the definition of "economically disadvantaged" will be out of luck if they do not fall within the defined underrepresented and substantially underrepresented industry groups. Then again, the SBA could determine that women-owned small businesses have been substantially underrepresented across all industries thereby resulting in a program which is essentially available to all women-owned small businesses.

Under the proposed 8(m) regulations, women-owned small businesses would have to submit an application for certification to the SBA. The new law states that criminal penalties apply if false statements are made in applying for the preference program. A better solution to the costly application process would be to have the women-owned small business owner sign a notarized certification attesting to the company's size and the owner's net worth. The self-certification document should specifically confirm that the party making the certification fully understands the penalties for false statements. A great deal of red tape and delay would be avoided if self- certifications were allowed.

Subcontracting with Prime Contractors

Prime contractors are required by law to subcontract certain portions of their work to small and small disadvantaged businesses. This is a major element in the federal government's small business advocacy program and, like the preference programs described above, it works.

The majority seem to believe that mandatory subcontracting is a good approach but small businesses beware. There is an inherent flaw in the system in that prime contractors agree to use small business on paper but do not do so in practice. It is not surprising that prime contractors operate in such a manner as to preserve their own self interest. The way to keep the primes honest is to force the prime contractor to sign an airtight teaming agreement which obligates the prime contractor to send small companies the work outlined in the bid proposal.

Most small businesses start out in the federal market by serving as subcontractors to federal prime contractors. These companies are forced to do so because they don't have the closing mechanisms discussed in previous chapters. Perhaps more importantly, most likely didn't know about GSA Schedule contracts until they had been in the game for six months or more.

Selling services and solutions to a prime contractor can be as frustrating as selling directly to federal agencies. The primes usually have a plethora of varying types of small businesses under their umbrella and making cold calls to a prime contractor can be a difficult process. Your first task is to find the key decision makers in the organization and most are buried deep within the inner layers of the prime's bureaucracy. If your primary contact directs you to the prime contractor's Diversity Department or Small Business Advocacy Group, you have been given the kiss of death. These departments will ask you to submit your capabilities statement for entry into their small business capabilities database. Your proffered statement will most probably wind up in the department head's circular file and it is not likely that you will hear back from that prime.

In contrast, there may be limited scenarios under which the prime contractor will welcome you with open arms. They are as follows:

1. Your sales staff has sold your company's services to an end user at a military base near your hometown. The end user wants to do business with your company and has money to spend. You don't have a closing mechanism, such as a GSA Schedule contract, so the base referred you to the contract manager for their favorite prime contractor. Under this scenario, the prime will embrace your company because you have brought an unforeseen opportunity to its attention and also because it will make a handsome profit by marking up your fees and costs.

2. You have a unique capability that the prime contractor needs and therefore can't find elsewhere.

3. Someone in your network of contacts knows a decision maker in the prime contractor's organization and has made a strong referral for you.

Beginning as a subcontractor to a prime is a good way to get your foot in the door because it is fast and relatively painless. The major drawbacks are that the prime contractor will try to insulate your company from the customer, take credit for your staff's superior performance, and attempt to grab the bulk of any new work you uncover. Although at first glance this may seem to be a gross injustice, your business will most likely do th same when it becomes a prime contractor.

The Use of Preference Programs by Prime Contractors

It is not uncommon for a large prime contractor to act as a subcontracto to a small business which has won a federal contract through one of the government's preference programs. In the situation described above, the terms of the federal contract will most likely specify that at least fifty percent of the contract's personnel costs must be spent on work performed by employees of the prime contractor (the small business) or personnel of other small businesses. This stipulation is in place to keep prime contractors from using small businesses and preference programs as fronts when closing sales. Large prime contractors may legally participate in small business preference contracts as long as this stipulation is strictly adhered to. Detractors say that in spite of the fifty percent rule, the small business is still a front for a large business. All in all, the practice works in favor of small businesses so the rules are not likely to change.

Large prime contractors maintain "stables" of different types of tested small businesses for use should a need arise. They have a thick Rolodex stocked with the names of small businesses, small disadvantaged business veteran-owned small businesses and the like. Nonetheless, a small business should take great pains to inform the primes of its preference status. Keep in mind that the primes are a tough sell because they already have hundreds of preference partners. On the other hand, doing business with a prime becomes a slam dunk if you have federal business in hand and are looking for a prime to help you close the deal. Imagine how high the prime contractor will jump if the end user, its valued and prized customer, has told the prime that she wants to do business with you.

Go After Small Opportunities in Your Locale

Small businesses do reasonably well within the Beltway because of the vast amounts of money available for contracts in the region. However, the overabundance of contract opportunities is offset by the level of competition. The Washington metropolitan area is home to the very largest prime contractors and small businesses are playing in their backyard. Small businesses hoping to do business near the Beltway must learn to play nice with the large primes or they run the risk of being shut out of the market.

Many small businesses emerge and prosper by staying close to home where the competition is not as intense. There are countless federal facilities located throughout the U.S. and overseas. Such facilities include military bases, research centers, Veterans Administration and military hospitals, and regional offices of various federal agencies. Take a peek at your local blue page telephone directory or peruse the federal agency web sites for contacts. Federal facilities located outside of the Beltway prefer, for political and social reasons, to work with local companies. Local businesses are also perceived by federal officials to be more cognizant of delivering value. It is not uncommon for a small business owner to meet an end user from a local federal facility at a social occasion or at a networking event. He or she can then turn the contact into a relationship and ultimately a sale.

Entering the Market

We are frequently asked, "What procedures should be followed by small businesses eager to participate in the federal market?" The answer to this question is that a small business should implement an aggressive federal sales program and simultaneously work toward obtaining a GSA Schedule contract. The latter should be of highest priority. A Schedule contract is the only practical way a small business can obtain a pre-approved price list under a multiple-vendor contract.

Many of the GSA Schedule solicitations covering services require that a company demonstrate that is has the background or corporate experience necessary to provide the services it is offering to the government. This presents a problem to new companies that have no corporate experience to draw upon. However, select GSA Schedule solicitations allow a company offering services to proffer the experience of management with a previous employer as the corporate experience required under that Schedule's solicitation. Start-ups hoping to offer products to GSA also face a hurdle because GSA requires that a company submitting an offer prove that it has sold the product in the commercial marketplace. Either of these factors can impact upon the time at which your company may submit its GSA Schedule offer.

What do you do while you are waiting to submit your GSA offer or are waiting for a submitted offer to be evaluated? The offer evaluation process can take three to nine months so you have plenty of time to do other things. We suggest that your company undertake the following steps:

1. Immediately begin an aggressive sales program to sell directly to federal end users. Do this on Day 1.

2. Provided you qualify, apply for small disadvantaged and/or service-disabled veteran-owned status. Prepare your application and get it submitted within the first thirty days.

3. Try to work through prime contractors to obtain subcontracts as the way to close your sale.

4. Use credit card transactions (under $ 2,500) or purchase-order transactions (under $ 25,000) to close your sales and get your foot in the door.

5. For deals that exceed $ 25,000, tell the federal customer that you are working on your GSA Schedule offer or that it has been submitted and it is in the evaluation stage. Larger deals take six to twelve months to sell so your GSA Schedule contract could be awarded by the time you are ready to close the deal. If it isn't, knock on the door of the prime contractor serving the agency.

6. Even if you fit within the parameters of one of the small business preference programs, approach selling to the government as if you didn't have such a status. Sell aggressively and effectively. Then use your preference edge to help close the deal. Get started today. Start making sales calls as soon as possible.

Chapter 12

Writing Federal Proposals

The CEO of a company announces in an e-mail message sent to all personnel that the company will be writing a large proposal for submission to the federal government and that the win is going to put the company on the federal map. The e-mail states: "I am sure that you will all be very excited to assist us in taking the company to a new level in federal contracting. Please send me an e-mail me if you would like to take part in this important endeavor."

Later that day, the CEO checks his e-mail for responses and there are none. He calls his information technology department and says: "Where is Jim? My e-mail is not working." Response: "Jim rushed out earlier stating that he has decided to take some time off."

The process of writing proposals is the Achilles heel of the federal solutions business. Even those companies that excel at writing them consider it a necessary evil. Federal proposal writing is an inherently complex and chaotic process. It is an expensive and risky game that neither the government nor the vendor really wants to play but must in the interests of competition and getting the best bang for taxpayer dollars. The game must be played by the government's rules, and this requires a highly structured and systematic process.

The process must begin with the vendor establishing a strong customer relationship and everything in the proposal must be based on that relationship. Newcomers incorrectly believe that a winning proposal can be crafted without first knowing the customer.

Why Proposals Exist

Why do proposals even exist? Contrary to popular belief, proposals are not written so federal evaluators can read thousands of pages of vendor proposals and finally, after weeks of proposal review, select the best, high value solution to their problem. In reality, proposals are written because the FAR requires actual documentation that a competition was held.

Why aren't proposals used to find the best solution? The answer lies in the fact that, in most cases involving the sale of services, the decision on the eventual contract winner was made far in advance of the time the proposal was written. End users usually want a proven incumbent contractor back in order to limit any disruption in operations. However, the agency is required by law to hold public competitions for selected procurements. In this situation, the winning company has to write a defensive proposal to protect its pre-established position with the customer.

Does the contracting officer care about the number of trees that went into the losing proposals? Maybe if he or she is an environmentalist but not really in most cases. The contracting officer's job is to follow the rule and the rules outweigh the concern for the trees. It's a rare case that an unknown slips in and unseats the favorite.

Has the winner always been predetermined? No. However, don't lie awake at night counting the revenue that you are going to receive from blind bids. You might win a small percentage but you will spend way too much money writing losing proposals and, equally importantly, burn out your staff in the process.

Is there a better solution? Multiple award contracts like GSA Schedules are a partial solution but don't look for revolutionary solutions anytime soon. The political pressure to keep up an appearance of competition is too intense.

Proposal Structure and Content

Most federal proposals have six parts. Total page counts can range from thirty to three thousand or more with the length of proposal depending on the complexity of the product or solution being sought. The chart below outlines the main components of a proposal.

Part	Number of Pages	Critical Elements
Executive Summary	1 – 2	Outlines why your company would provide the best service
Technical Approach	10 to 1,000 pages, depending on project size and government page limitations	Describes the customer's preferred solution; this is where most proposals are won or lost
Management Plan	10 to 100 pages, depending on project size and government page limitations	Describes how the contract will be managed and performance will be evaluated
Corporate Experience	10 to 30 pages, depending on the number of project descriptions required	Describes relevant corporate experience in the form of project summaries of 1 -2 pages in length
Personnel	5 to 300 pages, depending on the government's specifications for submission of staff resumes	Resumes of key persons designated to perform the work requested
Business Proposal	5 to 500 pages, depending on the complexity of the requirement	Pricing spreadsheets and related business documentation

The federal government has, within the past several years, started placing strict page limitations on some sections of proposals. The implementation of this policy has had a direct impact upon proposal preparation costs and has saved countless trees.

Conversely, the government is now requiring vendors to jump through hoops because it doesn't have the time or resources to check a particular vendor's references. In the old days, a company submitted a description of its relevant experience and the name and contact data for the person responsible for contract performance. The government would then call the reference to determine how the company performed. Apparently, this process was too cumbersome for the government to continue.

Under today's rules, the company must fill out a performance questionnaire, deliver it to the person cited in the proposal as a reference, arrange to get an original signature from the reference, and put the signed questionnaire in their proposal. Proposals that are submitted without the completed reference questionnaires are marked "nonresponsive" and are summarily rejected.

Why is Proposal Writing So Difficult?

Proposal writing is a dreaded chore not so much because it's difficult to generate the content, but because most people simply don't like to write. When the word goes out that your management intends to respond to a proposal, look under the desks for your technical people. They are hiding. Even the rare birds who like to write tend to postpone writing tasks because writing is hard work. Adding to the dilemma is the fact that your technical people have to be taken off billable work, which they actually like, to write, which they don't.

Writing a proposal is a very costly process. To do it well, a company must have a proposal manager with extensive experience and good writing and management skills. It also helps if your proposal manager has patience and is calm in the face of a storm. Gandhi or Mother Theresa immediately come to mind. Such traits are difficult to find in one person.

The proposal manager usually can't write the technical approach chapter. Drafting one requires the participation of technical specialists, the majority of whom don't necessarily write well.

Owners and managers of federal contracting companies view proposal writing as a necessary evil because:

- The process is hectic and it never seems to go smoothly.

- It's exceedingly expensive and the expense is compounded by the fact that people working on the proposal cannot bill their time on existing projects.

- Owners and managers, like others in the company, don't like to write or review proposals.

- It is a high-risk game and the chances for success are often low.

Writing a proposal often involves a series of chaotic events culminating in a last-minute crunch the day (and night) before the proposal is due. Even if you have a proposal manager who can produce the majority of the proposal, a large part of the job is heaped upon the technical people to produce the critical technical approach chapter. Most proposals win because of a customer-centric, compelling technical approach. It is therefore not surprising that those drafting the technical approach are usually at the center of the chaos.

Although proposal organization, management, and production can be contracted out to specialists, the customer-related sections of the proposal must come from the company's sales organization. Successful government contractors develop an in-house proposal writing capability and wean themselves from the outside specialists.

What Wins and What Doesn't

Generally, a company's likelihood for success on a contract bid is based on the company's relationship with the customer and the extent of its sales efforts prior to a Request for Proposal being issued.

Strength of Customer Relationship	Proposal Quality	Result
Strong seeing as you are the only vendor who made a meaningful connection with the customer	A+ -- meets all requirements and describes a solution that the customer wants	You win
Strong but so are the customer's relationships with several other competitors	A+ -- meets all requirements and describes a solution that the customer wants	You are in a dog fight and the winner is the vendor with the superior solution
Strong	B -- meets most requirements but lacks a creative, customer- centric solution	You risk losing and wasting you sales investment
Weak or nonexistent	B minus - - meets all requirements but lacks a customer-centric solution because you don't know the customer	You lose unless you are very lucky

Writing Proposals

Proposals written in response to a federal Request for Proposal are sales closing documents. A successful proposal is not written to win, it is written not to lose. It seems contradictory but it's true. Well-drafted proposals defend the sales beachhead that you have already established with the customer. They close deals that were sold earlier in the sales cycle.

Proposal writing is the last critical step in the sales process. The entire process - - from opportunity identification to customer relationship building to proposal writing and contract award - - should be one, highly-structured process.

An integrated sales and proposal process will result in a proposal that (i) presents a solution the customer wants, (ii) has all of the elements required by the government, and (iii) is completed well ahead of the submittal deadline. A haphazard process usually results in a writing crisis encountered just prior to the proposal's deadline, poor proposal quality, and a noncompliant proposal that winds up in the circular file.

The Secret: Write Fewer, Win More

An old adage in the sales business says: "Only sell to those who are ready to buy what you sell." Translated to proposal writing, the adage might be: "Only write winning proposals." Trite but true. Writing too many proposals results in a cascading series of negative events.

- You lose more because you can't maintain quality while writing numerous proposals at once.

- Staff morale goes down.

- Costs go up.

- Billable time and profits go down.

So how do you know which ones to write? Assess the strength of your customer relationships. Sometimes that will be easy and sometimes not. It can be hard to quantify the strength of a relationship, the extent to which your competitors have been pre-selling, and whether you have advocates or detractors within the agency.

The Bid/No Bid Decision

Making the bid/no bid decision is the single most important step in the sales process. You must bid wisely and selectively. Failure to do so is costly and demoralizing.

Many proposal experts believe that the bid/no bid decision should be made just before or concurrent with issuance of the Request for Proposal. In practice, the decision can be made much earlier in the sales process, often within the first several weeks of opportunity identification. At the latest, make the decision within three days of issuance of the Request for Proposal. In fact, the decision should probably be not to submit a bid if you haven't made a decision by the time the Request for Proposal is issued. Postponing the decision puts everyone in limbo and wastes valuable resources.

The more aggressive your preliminary sales efforts, the more likely that the bid/no bid decision will become obvious early in the process. Most managers and senior sales people develop a feel for your company's likelihood of success as intelligence is gathered. They document their sales intelligence as they go, both formally and informally. They apply their experience, instincts and "street smarts" when making tentative bidding decisions early in the process.

Bid/No Bid Guidelines

Strongly consider passing on a bid opportunity if one or more of the following are true:

- Customer relationships are nonexistent or weak.

- There is an incumbent and you do not know if the customer wants them back or not.

- You know the customer prefers another company.

- You do not have a solution to the customer's problem.

- You have any doubts about your chances of success.

Lean toward a no bid if:

- Your customer relationships are solid but you know they are talking with others and you are not sure what they think of your company or the competition.

- You do not know who wrote the Request for Proposal or who is on the evaluation committee.

- You are unsure of, or fear, a competitor.

- You think the sales staff may not be as close with the customer as they claim.

- You have any doubts about your chances of success.

- You know that others have been selling aggressively and there are players that are larger than your company.

- Too much outside recruiting is required.

- It is a stretch financially or strategically.

Bid if:

- Your customer relationships are strong.

- You know the customer's hot buttons and have the solution they want.

- There is an incumbent contractor, you know the end user does not want them back, and you have a relationship with the customer.

- You can significantly lessen the customer's concerns.

- You believe that the customer wants your company.

- You have a good sense that the customer is open to selecting your company.

- You have enough support to swing the evaluation with an excellent proposal.

An article by Jay Herther in the Spring/Summer 2006 Issue of the Journal of the Association of Proposal Management Professionals (APMP.org) says it all:

"If you use the concepts and tools in this article, you can avoid a dreaded customer debriefing quote: 'Sure, I'll tell you why you lost, if you tell me why you bid.'"

To summarize some of the key bid/no bid principles:

- Avoid blind bids.

- Have you positioned yourself to win by clearly articulating the customer's problem and your proposed solution?

- Have you addressed the customer's fears and do you have a convincing case that, by choosing your business, the customer will minimize his or her risk?

- Bidding on losers wastes resources and demoralizes the team.

- Remember that you can't focus on every opportunity. Focus your energy and critical resources on qualified and winnable opportunities.

Mr. Herther's article also provides the following sage advice:

"Instead of getting enticed into bidding a real long shot, the organization is better served by positioning to win the next opportunity. Go meet with the next customer. Go influence the requirements specification ahead of the RFP release. Go put together a demonstration to show the customer/ evaluators. Get prepared for the next one. Start a blitz of future visits to customers who will be releasing an RFP. Get ahead of the next opportunity."

Learn How to Fold'em

Texas Hold'em, a popular poker game, is currently sweeping the country. Many writers are drawing analogies between the game and business.

One of the most critical strategies of the game is to avoid playing hands that have a low probability of winning. Players ignore this advice and play such hands because they want to be part of the action rather than sitting out a hand twiddling their thumbs. Marginal hands are also played because most of us rely heavily on hope. Playing marginal hands slowly drains a player of chips, a poker player's lifeblood, leading to discouragement, and even worse decision making.

How does this relate to proposal writing? A CEO is told of a large procurement advertised in FedBizOpps, the central federal bid posting web site. At the beginning of his career, the CEO did Oracle development and still fancies himself as an Oracle expert. The procurement is being advertised by an obscure DOD intelligence agency that the sales staff does not know. The CEO announces at the weekly sales meeting, "This is made for us; let's go for it." The lead salesperson replies, "But we don't know anything about these people." The reply: "No matter; we are the leading Oracle development shop in the federal sector." As you may have surmised, this is a marginal hand.

The chips that will undoubtedly be wasted are billable time in the form of the dedication of the company's most valuable staff to days and weeks on end of proposal writing. These unlucky souls will have to devote substantial work and personal time on a losing effort. As could have been expected, the CEO's company loses the bid, discouragement sets in with his staff and the general corporate morale goes down. You can only go to the well so many times. The proposal that you wrote to win a re-bid of a large contract you already hold suffers and you lose that contract as well.

The Ego Bid

The above scenario is called an "ego bid." Every company has a corporate ego of some sort. Executives boast of being best of the breed and superbly qualified. A strong ego is, on some levels, a necessity because it drives a company to success. But remember that being superbly qualified in the services sector only means that you will go up against other superbly qualified companies. And they may have a long-standing relationship with the customer and you don't. Or the customer wants zero risk and the competitor is not only superbly qualified but is also a well-known giant prime contractor.

The best way to avoid "ego bids" is to recognize the phenomenon and consciously guard against it. Have a checklist for bid/no bid decisions and make a note on it to look at the decision from a corporate ego perspective. Are we doing this just because we think we are the best? Or do we really know the customer and have a high probability of winning?

Wild Cards Can Fool You

Every once in a while the stars will align correctly and a company will win a blind bid, called "wild cards." Consider a wild card bid if:

- Your company is writing no other proposals at the time.

- Your company is very qualified to meet all the requirements of the Request for Proposal.

- A win would meet a critical strategic goal of the company.

Our advice to avoid blind bids is a general rule and there are exceptions to every rule. Wild card bids should be rare and done with your eyes wide open. Understand that you are writing a proposal that probably won't win. Also keep in mind that winning a wild card bid can be dangerous. Sales people want to bid on every opportunity; their jobs depend on winning and they have a tendency to be overly optimistic. Most experienced proposal managers only want to write "guaranteed" winners based on customer relationships. These opposing positions surface in almost every bid/no bid decision. A wild card win can tip the scale toward bidding on all long shots. The sales manager might argue for a blind bid saying, "Remember that contract we won with DOE" while failing to mention that the win was five years ago and there have not been similar wins since that time.

Wild card bids are fine as long as you know that's what you're doing. Poor bidding decisions will drain your company and you could easily find yourself on a downward, losing spiral. Adhere to the advice provided above and you will find your corporate path to success will be much less bumpy.

Write Defensive Proposals

A defensive proposal is one that is:

- Written with the goal of being the last proposal standing

- Presents a practical solution from the customer's perspective

- Gives the customer what they want and no more and no less

- Addresses each and every requirement of the Request for Proposal

- Proposes a clear, concise solution, devoid of sales puffery

In short, a defensive proposal succinctly and effectively defends the position that you have already taken with the customer.

Ideally, you have met with the customer, identified his or her requirements, and proposed a solution that meets their needs. A successful proposal demonstrates that your company can back up what your sales staff said it could do. In other words, you close the deal with prose and provable facts and assure the customer that he will minimize his risk by going with you. You may have sold one or more of the people on the evaluation committee in advance of the proposal's submission. Now you sell the rest.

Don't bid if you haven't established a position to defend. You can count on the fact that one or more vendors have established positions. You will hear your salespersons lament that they can't get to the customer because there are too many competitors trying to do the same thing. Welcome to the world of direct sales and hard knocks. You have to get through the flack or not play in the market.

Process versus Content

Proposal writing involves both process and content. Effective processes are important but proposal content rules over process. Your company may develop a proposal smoothly, with minimal hassle and without last-minute crises, and submit a product that is beautifully formatted with fancy graphics. Yet the end result may still be that it loses due to lack of "responsive content."

A proposal that has been deemed to provide acceptable responsive content is one that contains all of the content or information asked for in the Request for Proposal and no more or no less. More importantly, the content must be presented in a concise manner and should demonstrate how your proposed solution is going to solve the customer's problem (or otherwise address his or her needs). This, of course, begs the question of how a business discerns what the customer wants. The answer to this query is that you can only do so through aggressive sales and the use of the customer intelligence gathered during the sales process.

Defensive proposals present an easily understood and direct solution which addresses the requirements outlined in the Request for Proposal. The information is presented in a clear and concise manner and is substantiated with provable facts presented without embellishment.

Proposal evaluators report, without exception, that a proposal should not gild the lily. More specifically, they state that a proposal should not contain:

- Unsubstantiated sales pitches

- Fancy bindings, graphics, and tab systems

- Information that was not requested in the Request for Proposal

Evaluators are intelligent, hard-working people who want to simplify their tasks. Extraneous information will not have the intended impact. In fact, it actually works against you because it makes the evaluator work harder to discern your message. Graphics can be used but only if the graphic makes the presentation clearer and more concise. Do not add graphics in an attempt to impress the reader.

Evaluators tell us that if they ask for two resumes, they mean two resumes. When they ask for three descriptions of past experience, provide the three requested. Resist the temptation to provide six under the theory that providing additional project descriptions makes you look deeper in experience and more capable.

We previously stated that providing a compelling technical approach is the key to a winning proposal. You can create a good technical approach using traditional outlining techniques, storyboards, and the development of effective selling points (customer solutions).

Implementing an Effective Business Process for Proposal Writing

Companies serious about developing quality proposals must develop an effective business process that integrates proposal writing with the sales process. The critical steps in developing a successful sales and proposal writing process are as follows:

1. Have top management actually get seriously involved in the writing of the proposal. Recognize that immense waste has occurred if less-than-stellar proposals go out the door. Submitting winning proposals can have a major impact on revenue and the survival of a federal services company.

2. Integrate the sales and proposal-writing process. We have previously mentioned the importance of this component.

3. Hire an experienced, full-time proposal manager who has mastered the art of minimizing the chaos. It is essential to make sure that your proposal manager likes to write and edit rather than just manage.

4. Implement a structured, documented and automated proposal-writing process.

5. Invest in building a database of up-to-date resumes and summaries of your corporate experience and actually keep it updated. The proposal manager can oversee this provided he or she has the right software. However, management must implement the right carrots and stick to actually get the technical staff to do it.

6. Automate and "version control" your old proposals and management plan boilerplate. Once again, the proposal manager can do this but management must invest in effective software and staff support to accomplish the task.

7. Write the executive summary before the proposal kickoff meeting. Make sure that it includes winning themes and salient selling points. The person who drafts the executive summary should be the sales or management person who knows the customer best. We suggest tackling this task ahead of time even if the first draft of the executive summary is only an outline with critical selling points as bullet points.

8. Use an incentive system to compensate your best technical writers when you win. I can feel you cringing about this one but it works. After all, why do most of us come to work? Yeah, I know it's the creative challenge but money helps.

In summary, proposal writing is probably the most dreaded task in federal sales. Everyone seems to hate it just like you probably hated term papers in college. To do it right and win, you have to write selectively and produce a quality proposal that reflects an intimate knowledge of the customer and the government's requirements. This, in turn, requires that sales and proposal writing be thought of as one process. Help the customer identity the problem and the solution as early as possible in the procurement process. Ideally, this occurs before the customer knows they have a problem and before the competitors arrive on the scene.

Chapter 13

Congress Controls the Game

A Report on the Forum on Acquisition, prepared by the Government Accountability Office, concluded that the federal government is on a burning platform caused by budget limitations clashing with national priorities. GAO determined that the federal government must develop new and innovative approaches to conducting the business of government. The time is now to transform federal procurement.

The FAR is one of the more egregious examples of congressional micromanaging run amuck. It is a patchwork of convoluted regulations resulting from laws designed to solve specific problems or serve specific political objectives. The laws and procurement regulations cry out for simplification.

Three specific congressional actions can be taken immediately to open the federal market and increase competition. Then Congress should clean the slate and start over with a new procurement law and a new FAR.

Let the Light Shine In

A huge problem that newcomers face when trying to enter the federal market place is that it is enormously difficult to find end users.

A centralized database providing information on existing contracts would go a long way toward opening the competitive process. In September, 2006 Congress passed a new law that requires the creation of a public contract awards database. Ideally, the new database would provide a summary of what was purchased and who the end users and official buyers are for each awarded contract. This new law would be the single biggest step ever taken to open the federal market.

GSA operates a similar database which is controlled by a contractor. The current database is virtually useless, primarily because the data is not timely and does not tell a vendor what product or service was procured.

Trying to piggyback a new database on the back of the current one would likely result in years of delay and would produce an ineffective, inefficient patchwork of incompatible data entry and search software programs. The current database should be operated until a brand new system is fully operational, at which point the old one should be consigned to the database graveyard.

In an ideal situation, the database would be developed from within GSA. The project will probably have to be contracted out but the contractor should not be allowed to control the data (as is the case with the current database). In other words, the contractor should not have any rights to the awards data whatsoever.

New regulations implementing the database law must have rigid and unbending rules about publishing contract awards. The three most important issues that need to be addressed are:

- Contracting officers should be required to post all new contract awards of more than $25,000 within 24 hours of award.

- A summary of what was purchased and the place of contract performance should be part of the record. The bureaucracy will resist publishing a summary of what was purchased; they will turn to "coding systems" rather than a simple description.

- The names of the end user of the product or service and the contracting officer should be published. Full contact data for the contracting officer (the telephone number, e-mail address, and mailing address for that person) should be included.

Neither the bureaucrats nor the federal contractors want a public award database; particularly if it shows the name of the end user of the product and service. Publishing end user information will meet vehement bureaucratic resistance because end users and contracting officers would receive too many phone calls from companies trying to penetrate the federal market. But this is exactly what Congress would like to happen.

Contracting officers will argue that there can be many end users for a particular contract and this is often true. But the identity of the Project Officer or the Contracting Officer's Official Representative (the terms are used interchangeably) is part of the contract. This person should be identified in the new contract awards database.

Full and open competition is too expensive and inconsistent with the end user's motivation to minimize risk. Even contracting officers don't want too much competition; they just want to follow the rules and the rules are written to encourage contracting with insiders.

An effective, online contract award database is not the Holy Grail everyone is looking for in federal sales. There isn't one and the best that can be done is to allow everyone easy access to what has been bought in the past. However, an awards database with free, public access would open the $390 billion market to public scrutiny. It would go a long way toward creating a more level playing field for newcomers, particularly small businesses. And it would save billions of dollars in two ways. Taxpayer dollars would be saved due to increased competitiveness in the market. And it might make a dent in the pork-barrel projects that are larded onto each year's appropriations bills. Transparency is one of the few tools that can be used to improve efficiency and effectiveness in government.

Increase Procurement Staff

The federal government does not have enough contracting officers to keep up with the procurement workload. Steven Schooner, co-director of George Washington University Law School's Government Procurement Law Program, summed it up best:

> "In both gulfs, Iraq and Louisiana, Congress seems to be able to find money to send auditors and inspector generals onto the battlefield after the fact to bayonet the wounded. But nobody seems to find money to put Contracting Officers on the ground to do it right the first time."

(Washington Post, August 9, 2006)

Schooner's quote says it all. Congress can find money for pork-barrel projects and almost everything else under the sun, and there is much chest-thumping and vows of reform when the process comes up short. But the contract workforce crisis continues to worsen. Congress should act immediately to fund more contracting officer positions throughout the government.

Label Public Bids

Public bids should carry the following warning label:

> "This procurement is open to all responsible and qualified companies. Companies inexperienced with public bidding in the federal market should understand that many companies may have already met with federal personnel making this procurement and have presented their solutions in one-on-one meetings. Early communications between companies and purchasers are not only permissible under federal acquisition regulations, but encouraged."

Detractors will argue that such a statement will discourage companies from writing proposals and reduce competition. Experienced federal contractors and federal proposal evaluators will silently cheer and say this is long overdue. The time and dollars saved for vendors and federal end users would be enormous. Inexperienced companies now spend their hard-earned dollars writing unsuccessful proposals that never had a prayer. Federal evaluators spend countless hours reading and rejecting proposals they never wanted to receive. Let's be honest and encourage inexperienced bidders to have the early communications with end users and play the sales game successfully.

The Bridge to Billions

The subject of Alaskan Native Corporations (ANCs) has been discussed in previous chapters. These corporations can be awarded any federal contract without even an iota of competition. The result is that billions of federal procurement dollars have been funneled through ANCs. Contracting officers love contracting with ANCs because, in choosing to go with an ANC, the amount of work involved in the procurements is minimal. There are occasional press reports railing about abuses, but everyone involved seems to be following the rules as dictated by law.

Businesses with a cozy relationship with ANCs are getting rich. Senator Stevens, the sponsor of the ANC preference legislation, got the dollars he intended for his state. The only ones being hurt by the lack of competition in this arena are the taxpayers and the other small businesses that aren't allowed to compete for the work. If ANCs were forced to compete under the rules associated with other small business preference programs, there would truly be fair and open competition.

Start from Scratch

Congress should start with a fresh slate and write one comprehensive procurement law. The federal regulations interpreting that law should be written in a clear, concise and legible manner. The major themes in rewriting procurement law should be:

- The elimination of costly and confusing paperwork. The red tape should be replaced with simple self-certifications signed by a company's CEO and CFO. The key to a successful self-certification program is certification by the highest level executives, a stringent enforcement program, and stiff penalties.

- The elimination of outdated regulations that serve little purpose.

- The simplification of standard contract clauses.

- The simplification of trade agreement regulations.

- The improvement of contract labor laws.

Simplify and Save Taxpayer Dollars through Self-Certification

Current federal procurement regulations are not only complicated and lengthy but they also leave a lot of critical vendor issues gray or ambiguous. Fraud, bribery, and misrepresentation will always exist in federal contracting just as they do in the commercial sector. The trick is to minimize the problem.

A strong self-certification program could eliminate hundreds of pages of regulations. The regulations should clearly outline the legal ramifications associated with making false statements, require that the certifications be made in writing, and mandate that the self-certifications be signed by the vendor's CEO and CFO.

Honest government vendors do not fear the strong penalties that go hand-in-hand with self-certification. Honest vendors figure self-certification requirements cut paperwork and keep their competitors honest. It is also critical that the government enforce the penalties associated with making false certifications. Enforcement actions should also be made public in order to deter future infractions. Bad dreams about living in a cramped, two person prison cell go a long way in eliminating false certifications.

The following table outlines the instances in which self-certifications would be needed and identifies the parties who would sign the certifications.

Certification Requirement	Person Required to Certify
That the prices offered to the government are the lowest prices offered to any customer over a prescribed time period	CEO CFO
The resume of an employee proposed to provide services to the government is complete, current, and correct	Employee
The salary and qualifications of a service employee offered to the government meet the requirements specified in the government's request for quote	An officer of the company
A woman-owned business meets the ownership requirements of the new Woman-Owned Small Business Preference program	CEO of Woman-owned business
Small business size status	CEO

The implementation of a self-certification process concerning the lowest prices offered to any customer would probably have saved the government billions in Iraq and Katrina contracts.

Chapter 14

Reinstate GSA's Central Role in Procuremen

Congress should make GSA the federal government's central procurement agency and fund it adequately. Under this proposed course of action, GSA would then provide procurement services to all agencies and streamline contracting procedures. In the long run the American taxpayer would reap the cost savings that come with centralized purchasing.

Bureaucratic infighting is all about increasing your budget, your staff, and your programs. Infighting occurs whether you're providing school lunches, maintaining army bases, looking to cure cancer, or attempting to fly to the moon. Agencies battling to keep or expand their reach have taken to promulgating their own multi-vendor contracts instead of going through GSA.

The resulting thicket of overlapping and competing multi-vendor contracts has resulted in an enormous amount of duplication of effort an confusion among federal buyers and vendors. For example, NASA manages a GWAC that competes directly with the GSA Schedule for information technology products and services. NASA administrators believe their GWAC suits their needs better than the GSA information technology schedule.

Other agencies using their own multi-vendor contracts argue that they can obtain better pricing, that they have specialized needs not addressed by the GSA Schedules, or that their multi-vendor contracts provide "competition to keep GSA on its toes." Based on this logic, perhaps GSA should look into starting a space probe program to keep NASA on its toes.

GSA, as the name "General Services Administration" implies, was created with the thought that it would be the central procurement source for all federal agencies. Small businesses are being hurt by the proliferation of multi-vendor contracts because most are awarded to a relatively small pool of companies. The number of small businesses holding multi-vendor contracts is in the hundreds; the number of small businesses holding GSA Schedule contracts is in the thousands.

The taxpayer is being shortchanged because the government is not taking advantage of procurement reforms and GSA's buying power.

Despite being outdated and burdened by red tape, the GSA Schedule program is the most successful multi-vendor contract program in the history of the federal government.

GSA has contributed to the proliferation of other agency multi-vendor contracts by not simplifying and modernizing the GSA Schedules program. In GSA's defense, the agency is woefully understaffed. Congress should act to streamline and centralize multi-vendor contract procedures by providing the underlying legislation to reassert GSA as the federal government's central procurement agency. It must also provide the funding necessary to carry out the mission and gradually phase out other multi-vendor contract programs. The only competing multi-vendor contractor that should be spared is that offered by the Defense Logistics Agency, which purchases specialized defense products and material. This would take several years to implement but the process should start now. GSA has new leadership in place and is poised to assume its central role.

Reinventing the GSA Schedule Program

The GSA Schedule program is currently under fire. It was noted above that many of the program's procedures and requirements are outdated. GSA is struggling with organizational issues and recently GSA procurement violations have blown up in the press. The problems are serious but not insurmountable. The biggest problems are:

1. The regulations concerning vendor disclosure of discounting practices, procedures for determining fair and reasonable pricing, and auditing guidelines are extremely outdated. The discounting disclosure form required by GSA currently is so onerous that many vendors consider it an abomination and cite it as the reason why they elect not to seek a GSA Schedule contract.

2. Solicitation requirements and the applicable regulations concerning fair and reasonable pricing are not interpreted consistently by GSA contracting officers.

3. The solicitations for the various Schedule contracts are inconsistent, poorly written, and overly complex.

4. The defined scopes of work for the various Schedule contracts are overlapping and incomplete. This results in the unfair rejection of some proposals while other vendors can't find a Schedule that fits their product or service even though they're selling something the government needs and wants.

5. GSA pricing guidelines are completely out of touch with reality. GSA contracting officers are currently demanding that vendors offer GSA the lowest price charged to any customer regardless of the terms and conditions associated with the lowest-priced sale. This overly rigid interpretation of price evaluation policy runs counter to a vendor's rights to a reasonable profit.

GSA's inconsistent application of the rules and outdated regulations make doing business under a Schedule contract risky for vendors and also makes them leery of dealing with contracting officers. GSA's new management is aware of these problems and is in the process of an agency-wide reorganization that will include a program to improve customer service.

GSA Schedule Funding: Eliminate Vendor Fees

One quick and easy step toward reform would be to eliminate the fee associated with doing business with GSA, the Industrial Funding Fee. As aforementioned, this fee is .75% of each dollar earned through a vendor's GSA Schedule contract. In theory, it is charged to help the government cover administrative costs.

The implementation of GSA's fee has resulted in false economies. Vendors simply fold the Industrial Funding Fee into their prices, while tracking, collecting, and processing the fees adds considerably to the burden of bureaucratic paperwork.

The collection of the Industrial Funding Fee has had an unintended impact upon small business. GSA will not admit this publicly, but it would prefer not to have small businesses on GSA Schedules. The primary reason for GSA's sentiment is that small businesses do not generate enough funding fees to fuel the bureaucracy. By getting rid of the Industrial Funding Fee, the bias against small businesses would be eliminated.

Suggested Reforms

Congress should gradually phase out GWACs and the existing GSA Schedules program and implement a new multi-vendor contract for products. The new program should be managed by GSA, would always be open for bids, and the number of vendors eligible for receipt of award would be unlimited. The proposed contract should incorporate the following reforms:

1. The corporate qualification requirements for small business contracts should be less stringent than those for large businesses, with more emphasis on the experience of management and less on corporate experience. The "years in business" requirement should be one year, at most.

2. The current price evaluation regulations for product contracts should be eliminated and replaced with an online price adjustment model based on the average of the ten lowest prices offered to any customer during the vendor's last calendar quarter. The GSA price for a product would be discounted by five percent from the average of the ten lowest prices. The vendor's ten lowest prices would be posted quarterly to an online database and used to calculate a new GSA price. The pricing database would be confidential and for government use only. New prices would be uploaded automatically from the confidential pricing database to a new database that replaces GSA Advantage!, the current public database for GSA schedule prices.

3. The pricing approach outlined in Section 2 above would allow GSA's pricing model to continually adapt to market conditions, particularly in industries with fluctuating market prices. GSA may elect to use a different number than ten in averaging prices. More than ten would favor the vendor and fewer than ten would favor

GSA. Using only a company's single most favored customer is what GSA is trying to do currently and this approach is not practical or realistic.

4. The GSA discount of five percent would be standard for all vendors, eliminating the large disparities in the negotiating policie currently used by GSA contracting officers. Many will argue that the GSA discount should be different for different vendors. A standard discount approach is fair because the market conditions for a vendor (product volume, fluctuating prices, and non-GSA revenue) will be reflected in their ten lowest prices. Equally important, a standard GSA discount would eliminate the current inconsistencies in GSA price evaluation policies. Also, simplifying price evaluation procedures and auditing requirements will result in enormous savings in personnel costs.

5. The new program would require that each vendor submit a quarterly certification that the vendor's "ten lowest prices" are accurate and fully disclosed. There should also be strong penaltie associated with making a misrepresentation.

6. The "Price Reduction Clause," the GSA Schedule contract clause that requires vendors to reduce prices if they change their discounting policies or their pricing, should be eliminated. The need for GSA to audit vendor discounting policies would be eliminated by having an effective online price adjustment module and stringent self-certification requirements. Eliminating the Price Reduction Clause would also significantly reduce vendor fears of unfair audits, red tape, and government auditing costs.

7. The government should phase out the current GSA Schedule. In doing so, it should set a date after which new proposals would no be accepted and allow existing GSA Schedule contracts to expire at the end of their term. Under this proposal, existing GSA Schedule vendors would have the option of submitting abbreviated proposals to move under the umbrella of the new contract system. If such an election were made, GSA would terminate the vendor's existing GSA Schedule contract once it receives an award under the new program.

Many bureaucrats and vendors will resist change because this is what they do best. Their response will be that the suggested reforms will not work for all companies or that GWACs cannot be phased out because the agencies with GWAC programs have specialized needs. If GSA is given the money, the authority, and the time needed to gradually phase out existing and competing multi-vendor contracts, an open, competitive and cost effective procurement system can be built.

Chapter 15

Redefine Federal Service Contracting

The process used by the federal government to buy services does not reflect how services are actually purchased. It is, in fact, more of a game than any other federal buying process. The current service contracting process is bogged down by a quagmire of rules and subterfuges designed to create the appearance of full and open competition. Existing federal rules require hourly labor rates which can't be evaluated effectively. Furthermore, current rules have resulted in the misrepresentation of qualifications, inflated hourly rates and, on the other end of the spectrum, companies operating at rates that are too low to provide value. Price comparison of different vendors' hourly labor rates doesn't really take place any longer except in the rare instances in which a contract will be billed on a time and materials basis.

Federal rules for the procurement of services, as currently written, require the appearance of competition. The result is that vendors must submit unnecessarily complex and expensive proposals. Unfortunately for the vendors who spend vast resources on the preparation of proposals, the quality of a submitted proposal means little in the end.

The ultimate selection of a service provider is a subjective process requiring judgments on the part of end users concerning value and potential risks to the government. Consider the following when examining current procedures:

- Do you ask for a written proposal when selecting a heart surgeon?

- Are you concerned if the heart surgeon you want costs more?

- Is the person represented by a resume worth $90 per hour or $110 per hour because he or she is exceptionally talented?

End users make decisions when purchasing services based on face-to-face discussions with the vendor and the quality of the work the company has performed in the past for the end user. End users also rely on the opinions of other federal end users and the company's customers if the end user does not have experience with the company. Isn't that the way you would select the person who is going to cut into your chest? Under the current system, federal end users can't easily hire the company they want because the rules by which they must play aren't realistic. In the end, the end user usually gets the company he or she wants but only after jumping through hoops. Here's a novel concept; let's simplify the rules and make them consistent with reality.

Transform Service Contracting

Congress should authorize a new approach to service contacting by directing GSA to create a standard multiple award contract for services which is open to all companies. Companies would register their capabilities at a central, online database called the Federal Service Contract (FSC) web site. Vendors interested in participating in service contracts would enter the following data at FSC:

- As many as ten past performance descriptions for commercial or government projects for each category of service offered by the company

- Performance evaluations for each project provided (including reference contact information for each project)

- The number of full-time staff employed by the vendor

- The vendor's size status and any small business preference program certifications held, if applicable

- Commercial and federal revenue for the past twelve months

- Office locations and contact data

- An acknowledgement by the vendor's CEO that he or she agrees to comply with the terms and conditions of the standard service contract

- A certification by the CEO that all information entered in the FSC database is accurate and current

The standard, online service contract would:

- Specify strong penalties for misrepresentation of any facts

- Specify that the federal government will pay standard hourly rates for service personnel

- Provide specifications for categories of labor

- List a standard hourly rate for each labor category

- Contain standard federal contract clauses

- Provide electronic procedures for requesting proposals and making task order awards

Vendor capabilities and proposals would be evaluated by end users at the task order (requirement) level rather than when they register in the FSC database. The FSC database and the standard service contract would be used directly by end users to make service contract awards, with oversigh by the contracting office.

An end user with a service requirement would follow the following procedures:

1. He would define the requirement in a statement of work written in clear and concise manner and in a standard format, not to exceed 10 pages.

2. Three or more companies registered in the database would be invited to meet individually with the end user and contract stakeholders to discuss the work statement and define solutions. Additional face-to-face meetings and unlimited telephone and e-mail communications would be encouraged and permitted up to contract award. Companies that assist end users in defining work requirements would be required to register in the database as a condition of further communications.

3. The end user would request a technical proposal from three or more companies in the FSC database. The proposal would have to be provided in a standard, electronic format not to exceed ten pages. Oral presentations and live demonstrations could be

substituted for written technical proposals, at the discretion of end users.

4. Vendor proposals would, among other criteria, be evaluated based on the submitted resumes for key persons proposed for a task order. Resumes would be required to match the GSA standard labor category specifications. Individual employees would be required to certify that their resumes are accurate and correct. Contractors would be required to make resume certification part of employee training.

5. The end user would request an electronic, fixed-price bid based on standard hourly rates specified at the FSC web site. Time and material price bids would require the approval of the contracting office.

6. The end user would require that a corporate officer certify that the qualifications of the people assigned to a task order match GSA's labor category specifications. He or she would also be required to certify that employees assigned to a contract have certified the accuracy of their resume. Auditing would be eliminated by making it the Project Officer's responsibility to assure that the staff assigned to projects, their resumes and their performance match the GSA labor category specifications.

7. The end user would select the company receiving the award and make the award electronically.

8. It would be the end user's responsibility to prepare a written award justification not to exceed two pages. Vendor protests would be limited to procedural violations. Best-value determinations would not be subject to challenge.

Unlike the GSA Schedules program, there would be no fee associated with the new initiative. Rules could be put in place requiring the participation of more than three companies for large projects. Small business set-asides would be specified by the contracting office and small businesses would be invited to bid in the FSC database. Because small businesses may not have the same experience that larger contractors possess, the procurement officer should have the latitude to reduce the number of past performance descriptions required of small businesses.

The approach described in this chapter could potentially eliminate the need for contract labor laws. It would also eliminate the current contractor practice of invoicing unqualified personnel under a higher labor category and significantly reduce contract audit costs.

Setting Standard Prices for Services

As part of the FSC web site, GSA would establish an online database of labor category specifications and corresponding hourly prices. Labor category specifications would be developed using the Standard Occupational Classifications set by the Bureau of Labor Statistics (BLS) at http://www.bls.gov/search/soc.asp. Years of experience and education requirements would be added to the BLS classifications to expand the classifications into junior, mid-level, and senior categories for each classification.

GSA would establish an hourly rate for each labor category by using the average hourly rate established by the Bureau of Labor Statistics in the National Occupational Employment and Wage Estimates at http://www.bls.gov/oes/current/oes_nat.htm#b15-0000. GSA would add a standard price for each labor category to the database by multiplying the average hourly BLS rate by 3.0 to account for benefits, overhead, general and administrative expenses and profit. GSA would then establish a required salary range of ten percent on either side of the standard hourly rate and require that a corporate officer certify that each contract employee's wages falls within the range. The proposed certification would eliminate a big loophole in federal service contracting which is the practice of putting cheap personnel in the wrong labor category and invoicing the government for their services.

Fair and Reasonable Pricing

Opponents will argue that a standard direct labor multiplier of 3.0 will not accurately reflect vendor's actual price structures. Small businesses have direct labor multipliers as low as 2.0, medium-sized companies around 2.5 to 3.0 and the large prime contractors may go as high as 4.0. Setting a standard of 3.0 would presumably be unfair to those above 3.0 and a windfall to those below. However, a company operating at higher than a 3.0 multiplier is not operating efficiently. Small to medium-sized businesses operating under 3.0 could use the extra capital to pay better health benefits and invest in development of the company to better compete with the big guys.

The service contracting reforms outlined in this chapter eliminates many of the imperfections associated with the current system. End users, those persons whose jobs depend on the services procured, would control the process and make purchasing decisions much in the same way they do currently. But purchasing decisions would be made openly and quickly without any deception. Decisions would be made based on the end user's subjective evaluation of a vendor's capabilities, solutions and personnel. The end user would balance these factors with value and his or her perception of the risk involved. The proposed solutions would significantly reduce vendor costs and would improve the efficiency of the government's contracting personnel.

Chapter 16

Consolidate Small Business Preference Programs

Can you imagine what goes through a small business owner's mind when a federal official asks, "Are you a small HUBZone, disabled veteran, or 8(a) certified business?"

Reply: "I am not sure we are any of them but I did stay at a Holiday Inn Express last night."

Small business preference programs mystify companies outside the market. These programs seem straightforward to an insider but are a confusing puzzle for companies not experienced in federal contracting. The inexperienced have to determine which category they fall under while sifting through the maze of preference program regulations. The current list of categories is shown below and Congress adds to the list as politics dictate.

- Small businesses

- Socially and economically disadvantaged small businesses

- HUBZone small businesses

- Veteran-owned small businesses

- Service-disabled veteran-owned small businesses

- Woman-owned small businesses

- Woman-owned small businesses in an industry that is substantially underrepresented in federal contracting

- Woman-owned economically disadvantaged small businesses in an industry that is underrepresented in federal contracting

A company must read lengthy and often hidden regulations to determine whether it qualifies under one or more of these categories. To add to the confusion, the same company could qualify as "large" or "small" depending on what the government is purchasing at the time. The red tape associated with filing certifications and preference applications often scares companies away from the market.

Simplify Preference Programs Based on Social and Economic Status

All small business preference programs based on social and economic status should be combined into one program with quantifiable and specific certification requirements. As with reforms suggested in prior chapters, the filings of annual self-certifications would eliminate the need for the time consuming and expensive application process.

Simplify Business Size Standards and Set-Aside Programs Based on Procurement Size

Current regulations concerning small business set-asides and small business size standards are inconsistent and confusing. Both are based on North American Industry Classification System (NAICS) codes for the product or service being procured and, because of this, a business may be classified as small for a specific procurement and large for another. The size standards themselves are inconsistent and vary widely. Some size standards are determined by a company's average annual revenue and others by the number of employees currently employed by the contractor. The tables associated with government size standards are the size of a small book.

Regulations for procurement set-asides and business size standards should be changed so that they are not based on industry type and they assist businesses of various sizes. Contracting officers should be given the latitude to determine if a set-aside should apply to a particular procurement with said decision being based on end user requirements and the set-aside goals of an agency, not what is being procured. Contracting officers have the experience needed to determine the business size that is most appropriate for an individual procurement based on value and risk to the government and they should make set-aside decisions based on these considerations.

New Business Size Standards

Recommended business size standards are as follows.

Business Size	Size Standard: Average Annual Revenue for Last Three Fiscal Years Less Than	Set-aside Rule
Very Small	$1,000,000	All purchases under $100,000. Set-aside for very small businesses
Small	$10,000,000	All purchases from $100,000 to $500,000. Set-aside for small businesses
Medium	$100,000,000	Selected procurements over $500,000. Set-aside for businesses meeting medium size standard or less, at the discretion of contracting officers
Large	$500,000,000	Selected procurements over $500,000 set-aside for businesses meeting large size standard or less, at the discretion of contracting officers
Very Large	Greater than $500,000,000	None, full and open competition. Contracting officers would have discretion to set-aside selected contract for very large businesses only when the believe that contracting with a very larg business is in the interest of the taxpaye

Opponents to these recommended rule changes will most likely complain that they are too simplistic. But that is the beauty of the recommended rules. There is no reason for the complexities and confusion that current exists concerning small business set-asides.

Average annual revenue for the past three fiscal years should be used for all size standards because revenue is easier to verify, as opposed to employee counts, which can be difficult to quantify. Once a set-aside contract is awarded, the contractor would continue under that size standard for the full term of the original contract regardless of revenue growth during that time. The company's size standard would be re-visited at the beginning of any option period. Similarly, a contract would continue under the size standard if a contractor is acquired by a larger company for the full term of the contract, but not for option periods.

For multi-vendor contracts with terms of more than a year, a vendor should continue under the original size standard for twelve months after the end of the fiscal year that resulted in the vendor exceeding that size standard.

The SBA has been wrestling for many years with changing small business size standards and related regulations concerning how long a vendor can keep their size status for awarded contracts. Even by bureaucratic standards, the hand wringing and foot dragging are reaching a level beyond embarrassment. It's time for action.

Provide Contracting Officers with the Authority and Incentives to Meet Small Business Goals

Congress should force the SBA to make the following changes in policy:

1. Realistic small business set-aside goals should be established for agencies and contracting officers.

2. Contracting officers should be given the authority required to meet the goals and enforce prime contractor goals in their small business subcontracting plans.

3. Incentive programs which encourage contracting officers to meet small business goals should be implemented and contracting officers should be compensated when they do.

4. Make it the Project Officer's responsibility to ensure that prime contractor's meet their small business goals. These officials have the delegated authority to assess contractor performance. They are the individuals with knowledge of day-to-day contractor performance and they know which small businesses have actually been used as subcontractors.

The suggested reforms and incentives could potentially save millions of dollars. The recommendations in this chapter will curl the hair of many in the federal bureaucracy. The small business specialist/advocate program is like kudzu, the creeping vine. The programs are located throughout the federal system and each one acts to protect its self-interest. But ask any small business looking for an introduction to an end user with money about a small business advocate's usefulness. The answer is likely to range from not very to not in the least bit helpful.

Chapter 17

Improve the Current Procurement System

Federal procurement regulations, practices, procedures, and web sites are at best a mess; at least for companies outside the market. New regulations and patchwork fixes are frequently added to current convoluted and poorly-written regulations. A partial list of some of the problems associated with the current system includes:

1. The voluminous tome of bureaucratic rules called the FAR.

2. CCR, the government's central web site for contractor registration.

3. ORCA, the government's web site recently implemented for contractors to complete online representations and certifications. The 27 certifications required in the current web site are cluttered and outdated; certifications have been added over the years as a specific piece of procurement legislation is passed. Do we need several hundred thousand vendors certifying that they are not a Historically Black College or University? There has to be a better way. The ORCA web site and its required certifications are a prime example of the major problems associated with procurement regulations. The bureaucrats failed to clean up the certifications as the need for a particular one ceased to exist.

4. FedBizOpps, the centralized web site for publication of procurements and contract awards. The web site fails to provide an effective way to tie the public procurement announcement to the contract award (if and when an award is published).

5. The Federal Procurement Data System, an ineffective database for publishing contract award information.

6. The proliferation of GWACs and countless other multi-vendor contracts.

7. The large number of GSA Schedule contracts.

8. The existence of numerous multi-vendor contracts operated by the Defense Logistics Agency.

9. A tangled mess of small business preference programs covering nine different types of small businesses, each with different certification requirements, applications, and procedures.

And these are only some of the major issues. Although the federal bureaucracy is big, it doesn't have to be this complex. The procedures cry out for simplification.

Suggested Reforms: Implement a Simple Web Site for Doing Business with the Federal Government

The federal government has recently begun to simplify procurement red tape by implementing a web site called Acquisition Central (http://www.acquisition.gov/), an interagency endeavor created to integrate acquisition practices and procedures. Acquisition Central represents significant progress but it doesn't address all of the problems. Experienced federal contractors understand the different databases in Acquisition Central but outsiders do not. Ultimately, acquisition practices and procedures have to be centralized in one web site and Acquisition Central is a big step in the right direction.

Congress should require GSA to implement a single, user-friendly web site for vendor registration, vendor certification, bid publishing, bid receipt, and announcements of contract awards. The proposed web site should include procurement forecasts for all federal agencies. Call it "Business Central" and combine the registration and company representation and certification requirements into a single record with vendor help buttons written in plain English. GSA, not outside contractors or other government agencies, should operate the proposed Business Central web site.

Publish Procurement Rules for Laymen

Business Central should include a simple, easy-to-read explanation of how procurements are made. It can be done; tell your congressperson that this author volunteers to write the explanation free of charge and as a public service. Surprisingly, it can even be done in fewer than two thousand words. Imagine that! The proposed summary should, among other things, focus on how sales are closed and the realities of competing in the federal market.

Expand and Strengthen the Federal Credit Card Purchasing Program

The existing program which allows procurement officers to use federal credit cards is one of the most effective purchasing practices ever implemented in the federal government. It is particularly effective in stimulating purchases from small businesses. The program emulates commercial practices and it works. If a federal employee's computer monitor fails, the office administrator has a way to have it replaced the same day by a small business down the street.

Abuses by credit card holders have sullied the program somewhat and the bureaucracy moved in the wrong direction by curtailing some aspects of the program. Credit card charges for non-business trips to Vegas have been uncovered and, in many cases, the violations have gone unpunished.

The answer to the problem is improved management controls and stiff penalties for abuse, not watering down the program. Credit card programs will always have some degree of abuse because they involve people with the liberty to spend money. But, credit card abuse is a crime in the commercial sector and commensurate penalties are assessed. In the federal sector, taxpayer dollars are sometimes viewed differently from "real" money and federal employees stealing them are treated like naughty children. They get a slap on the wrist and nothing more.

Congress should strengthen the federal credit card purchasing program by:

- Encouraging the use of credit cards and increasing the purchase limit to $5,000

- Tightening standards concerning the parties to whom credit card privileges are granted

- Deducting the improper purchases from the offending federal employee's paycheck and terminating them once the sums have been paid back in full

Streamline Procedures for Small, Simplified Purchases

The threshold for small, simplified purchases should be increased from $25,000 to $50,000 and bids under $50,000 should no longer be published as public bids. Instead, a web site should be developed which can be used for purchases of less than $50,000. The web site should have an e-mail system which allows the contracting officer to solicit three bids from small businesses and also allows contracting officers to solicit bids using their own databases of small businesses (their list of local bidders).

Expand Emergency Procurement Procedures

More liberal rules concerning the level of competition required in emergency situations have been in effect for some time. The FAR was recently amended to provide contracting officers with greater flexibility when making emergency purchases. Such regulations have been invaluable when used in furtherance of the Hurricane Katrina recovery efforts and the Iraq war. Unfortunately, lawmakers did not anticipate, and the regulations accordingly did not address, the price gouging issues which arise during emergency situations.

The most important new emergency purchasing rule is:

"Agencies may limit the number of sources and full and open competition need not be provided for contracting actions involving urgent requirements."

The FAR should be amended further to provide contracting officers with a simple, straightforward contract for use in making emergency purchases. The proposed contract should require that the contractor's CEO and CFO both certify that the contract price for the product or service being purchased is the average of the five lowest prices charged any customer in the last sixty calendar days. Trust me; I will need to have my flack vest on when the federal contracting associations read this recommendation.

Chapter 18

Talk to Your Congressional Representatives

The recommendations in this book for improving the federal procurement system have three common characteristics:

1. The system must recognize how purchases are actually made in the federal market.

2. Procurement procedures should be simplified to reduce costs to citizens and vendors.

3. Fundamental changes must be made rather than improvements to current procurement practices.

4. There should be a focus on reducing price gouging and gray areas in contractor compliance.

The recommendations will not make the federal market fully open and competitive. As a practical matter, this would be impossible. However, they would dull the edge that insiders have currently, help small- to medium-sized businesses penetrate the market, and save the government billions of dollars by increasing competition.

Congress has to be involved in implementing the recommendations made. The bureaucrats in the Executive Branch will have a thousand reasons why change can't be implemented. Lack of funding will be one reason put forth. A conservative estimate suggests that opening the market to broader competition could produce annual savings of three to five percent from a $390 billion market. That's somewhere between $12 billion to $ 20 billion. The funds to implement the recommendations in this book would probably cost in the $60 to $100 million-dollar range. An $80 million investment to save around $16 billion sounds like a nice return of nearly two hundred percent. Any profit-motivated company would jump at it.

Others will argue that Congress has more important national priorities and this is probably true. What is a measly $16 billion; we spend that in just a couple of months in Iraq. This may seem like a reasonable counterargument, but we can't neglect fundamental management problems in government because of national politics. The government could bankrupt the country through mismanagement if we argue that Congress can focus only on major national priorities. Congress has to either make transformational level changes in procurement policy or delegate the authority to the Executive Branch.

Making fundamental changes in the procurement system is not that difficult. It would be easier to start from scratch than rewrite what exists now. Congress should use procurement experts to write legislation in clear, concise language that can be understood by people outside the government, and then provide adequate funding and practical implementation deadlines.

Readers who agree with any or all of the recommendations should take the following steps:

1. Send an e-mail to your congressional representative and include in the e-mail those recommendations outlined in this book that you have deemed of merit. Congressional e-mail addresses can be found at http://www.house.gov/writerep/ and http://www.senate.gov/general/contact_information/senators_ m.cfm. In order to make your task easier, we have reprinted our suggested reforms at http://www.fedmarket.com/procrecommendations. Ask your congressional representative for a reply to your email.

2. House and Senate members are inundated with e-mails from constituents and special interest groups. You will probably not receive a meaningful reply to your e-mail and you should then call the congressperson's Chief of Staff.

3. If the Chief of Staff does not talk to you, form a coalition of local companies through your Chamber of Commerce or a similar

group and call the congressperson's office and request that he or she meet with the group.

4. If all fails, consider the lack of response when you vote.

Let's be serious about fundamental changes in the procurement system and tell Congress to act. And your representative needs to understand that you know that passing legislation without adequate funding is the same as not acting at all.

Appendix I

Ordering Information

Recommendations to Congress

In Chapter 18, I recommended that you send an e-mail to your congressional representative concerning needed improvements to the federal procurement system. I further proposed that interested parties include in that e-mail message any recommendations of mine that they find are worthy of merit. A list of the recommendations is available in electronic form at http://www.fedmarket.com/procrecommendations.

Online Version

This book will be updated quarterly online to reflect changes in the federal market. Information will be presented in the following appendices to the online book.

1. Selling Services in the Federal Sector

2. The Sales and Proposal Business Process

3. Writing a Defensive Proposal

4. GSA Schedules

5. Selling at Federally-funded Research and Development Centers

6. Selling to the Department of Defense

To order this book over the internet, go to http://www.fedmarket.com/RollingDiceinDCOnline.

Audio Version of Book

An audio version of this book is available in downloadable MP3 format and on compact disc.

To order an audio version of the book, go to http://www.fedmarket.com/AudioBook.

Related Online Information:

Author's Blog: http://www.fedmarket.com/RollingDiceinDCBlog.

Fedbook: Visit our network created for federal salespersons to share sales experiences and advice. http://www.fedmarket.com/FedBook.

Seminars by the Author: http://www.fedmarket.com/RichardWhiteSeminars